Citizenship and the American Empire

Citizenship and the American Empire

Notes on the Legislative History
of the United States Citizenship
of Puerto Ricans

José A. Cabranes

New Haven and London   Yale University Press

1979

This book was originally published as an
article in the *University of Pennsylvania Law Review*
127 *U. Pa. L. Rev.* 391 (1978).

Published with assistance from the
John Hay Whitney Foundation

Set in Baskerville type.
Printed in the United States of America by
Halliday Lithograph Corp., Hanover, Mass.

Published in Great Britain, Europe, Africa, and
Asia (except Japan) by Yale University Press,
Ltd., London. Distributed in Australia and
New Zealand by Book & Film Services, Artarmon,
N.S.W., Australia; and in Japan by Harper & Row,
Publishers, Tokyo Office.

Library of Congress Cataloging in Publication Data
Cabranes, José A.
   Citizenship and the American Empire
   "Originally published as an article in the University
   of Pennsylvania law review,
   127 U. Pa. L. Rev. 391 (1978)."
   1. Citizenship—United States, 2. Citizenship—Puerto Rico.
3. Puerto Rico—Politics and government—
1898-1952. I. Title.
KF4720.P83C3   323.6'29   78-65479
ISBN   0-300-02325-1

Contents

For Susan Beth, Jennifer, and Amy

Preface

This study, begun while I was teaching at Rutgers University Law School in the early 1970s and long delayed by periods of public service and university administration, has a simple enough objective: to trace how, between the years 1900 and 1917, the Congress of the United States decided that the people of a distant colonial territory should be made American citizens.

The "legislative history" of a statute ordinarily is researched and invoked by lawyers for the limited purpose of aiding judicial interpretation. The object of statutory interpretation is "to determine the meaning which ought to be attributed to the statute as formally enacted"; in searching for the meaning of a statute, lawyers consider only those aspects of its legislative history "which were officially before the legislature at the time of its enactment."* I have tried to be faithful to this legal method by relying almost exclusively on records of Congress. However, the more general purpose of this particular exercise is to explain the legislative context within which was enacted the statute which so significantly shaped Puerto Rico's subsequent history.

This subject, long confused by polemics in Puerto Rico, deeply touches the sensibilities of all politically conscious Puerto Ricans. In writing a legislative history in the style (and, I hope, with the discipline) associated with American law reviews, I have sought to avoid unsubstantiated or speculative interpretations of textual materials and association of this research with personal political preferences concerning the status of Puerto Rico. I offer this editorial explanation, if not apology, especially to non-lawyers, who properly may be perplexed by a form of essay which relies so heavily on copious annotation.

My interest in the history of Puerto Rico I derive from my parents, Manuel Cabranes, born in Toa Alta, Puerto Rico, and Carmen López de Cabranes, born in Punta Santiago, Puerto Rico. Their longing for broadened opportunities for their children took them to New York City in 1946, where they experienced the trauma and alienation of earlier immigrants and where they learned to

---

* HART AND SACKS, THE LEGAL PROCESS: BASIC PROBLEMS IN THE MAKING AND APPLICATION OF LAW 1284 (tentative and unpublished ed. 1958).

survive, adapt, and prosper in new surroundings, while retaining always their love of their homeland.

I owe a debt of gratitude to my research assistant at Rutgers, Florence Ageitos, and my research assistants at Yale, Félix López, William Anthony Stewart, and Sonia Sotomayor de Noonan. Support for their labors, and mine, was made available by the John Hay Whitney Foundation, whose president and executive director, Archibald Gillies and Hugh Burroughs, were especially encouraging, helpful, and patient. I was much encouraged in my work by Edward Tripp, the editor-in-chief of the Yale University Press, whose broad-ranging interests (happily) included Puerto Rico and its people. Finally, I am grateful for the demanding and sensitive editorial efforts of Pamela Daley Kendrick, Sarah Helene Duggin, and John J. Sarchio of the *University of Pennsylvania Law Review,* in which this study first appeared.

New Haven, Connecticut
March 21, 1979

Citizenship and the American Empire

I. Introduction

The acquisition of Puerto Rico,[1] Guam, and the Philippines following the Spanish-American War signaled the rise of the United States to the position of a world power.[2] The American experience with empire was an important aspect of the global role assumed by this country following the "splendid little war" of 1898.[3] This imperial experience—intervention in Cuba [4] and occupation of the three former Spanish territories of Puerto Rico, Guam, and the

---

[1] Between 1900 and 1932, Puerto Rico was officially misspelled as "Porto Rico"—a result of the incorrect spelling of the island's name in the English version of the Treaty of Paris. Treaty of Paris, Dec. 10, 1898, United States-Spain, 30 Stat. 1754, T.S. No. 343. This incorrect spelling was later introduced into formal usage by the Foraker Act. Foraker Act (Puerto Rico), ch. 191, 31 Stat. 77 (1900).

During the debates on the Foraker Act, Representative William A. Jones of Virginia, who would later play a decisive role in shaping Puerto Rico's relations with the United States, claimed that the Senate had blotted out the island's true name "because, forsooth, some Republican politician, ignorant of its derivation and meaning, and insensible to the wishes and the feelings of those who are attached to it, had abitrarily [sic] and wickedly determined that it shall be so." 33 Cong. Rec. app. 233 (1900) (remarks of Rep. Jones). Jones aptly noted that Puerto Ricans had objected "that there does not even exist the pretext of changing the name to Americanize it, since porto is not an English but a Portuguese word." Id.

It took the Puerto Ricans 32 years to persuade Congress that the island should have its rightful name restored. Congress changed the island's name to "Puerto Rico" by joint resolution on May 17, 1932. Act of May 17, 1932, ch. 190, 47 Stat. 158 (1932).

Throughout this Article the author has used the correct spelling; for the sake of accuracy and convenience, however, quotations using the incorrect but then official spelling, "Porto Rico," are reproduced as originally printed without further notation.

[2] See F. Dulles, America's Rise to World Power 1898-1954, at 21-81 (1955): G. Kennan, American Diplomacy 1900-1950, at 4-20 (1951); J. Pratt, A History of United States Foreign Policy 201-38 (2d ed. 1965) [hereinafter cited as United States Foreign Policy]. See also J. Pratt, America's Colonial Experiment (1950) [hereinafter cited as Colonial Experiment]; J. Pratt, Expansionists of 1898 (1936) [hereinafter cited as Expansionists]; C. Woodward, Empire Beyond the Seas, in The National Experience 518 (2d ed. 1968).

[3] The Spanish-American War was called a "splendid little war" by John Hay, a leading expansionist of the time and United States Ambassador to England in 1898. In a letter to then Colonel Theodore Roosevelt of the Rough Riders, Hay wrote: "It has been a splendid little war; begun with the highest motives, carried on with magnificent intelligence and spirit, favored by that fortune which loves the brave." Letter from John Hay to Theodore Roosevelt, quoted in F. Freidel, The Splendid Little War 3 (1958).

[4] The United States purportedly intervened in Cuba to help secure the independence that the Cubans had fought for in two nationalist revolutions. 2 P. Foner, A History of Cuba and its Relations with the United States 162-275, 347-59 (1963); 1 P. Foner, The Spanish-Cuban-American War and the Birth of U.S. Imperialism xv-xxxiv, 1-150 (1972); 3 W. Johnson, The History of Cuba 145-336 (1920); C. Márquez Sterling, Historia de Cuba 165-244, 247-302 (1969); H. Thomas, Cuba: The Pursuit of Freedom 245-63, 316-27 (1971). President McKinley and proponents of American imperialism (such as Henry Cabot Lodge, Theodore Roosevelt and Alfred Thayer Mahan), however, transformed the war into a quest for empire. F. Dulles, supra note 2, at 34-36, 42-56; H. Morgan, America's Road to Empire 75-99 (1965); United States Foreign Policy, supra note 2, at 367-86; Colonial Experiment, supra note 2, at 58-64; Expansionists,

Philippines [5]—revealed in microcosm many of the characteristics of

---

supra note 2, at 231-32, 326-60; C. WOODWARD, *supra* note 2, at 525-34. *But see* 1 P. FONER, *supra,* at 208-310. The targets of this new American imperialism were the islands of the Spanish Empire in the Caribbean and the Pacific: Cuba, Puerto Rico, the Philippines, and Guam. A policy of forcible annexation such as was effected in Puerto Rico, Guam, and the Philippines was not possible in the case of Cuba because of the self-denying proclamations that accompanied the American call to arms.

On April 11, 1898, President McKinley sent an emotional and stirring message to the Congress announcing that American efforts to end the war between Spain and the insurgents in Cuba had failed. 55 CONG. REC. 3699 (1898) (President's message). After describing recent developments, the President appealed to Congress to intervene, stating that

> [t]he only hope of relief and repose from a condition which can no longer be endured is the enforced pacification of Cuba. In the name of humanity, in the name of civilization, in behalf of endangered American interests . . . , the war in Cuba must stop.

> . . . I ask the Congress to authorize and empower the President to take measures to secure a full and final termination of hostilities . . . , and to secure in the island the establishment of a stable government . . . , and to use the military and naval forces of the United States as may be necessary for these purposes.

Id. 3702. Congress acceded to the President's request, but not before his Democratic critics in the Senate managed to convince a majority to adopt a resolution providing "[t]hat the people of the Island of Cuba are, and of right ought to be, free and independent." H.R.J. Res. 233, 55th Cong., 2d Sess., 30 Stat. 738 (1898). Another "anti-imperialist" resolution was introduced and adopted at the request of an expansionist (*see* COLONIAL EXPERIMENT, *supra* note 2, at 395 n.27), Senator Henry M. Teller of Colorado. It provided "[t]hat the United States hereby disclaims any disposition or intention to exercise sovereignty, jurisdiction, or control over . . . [Cuba] except for the pacification thereof, and asserts its determination, when that is accomplished, to leave the government and control of the Island to its people." H.R.J. Res. 24, sec. 4, 55th Cong., 2d Sess., 30 Stat. 738 (1898). Senator Teller said that he had had the resolution introduced

> to make it impossible for any European government to say, "when we go out to make battle for the liberty and freedom of Cuban patriots, that we are doing it for the purpose of aggrandizement for ourselves or the increasing of our territorial holdings." He wished this point made clear in regard to Cuba . . . .

COLONIAL EXPERIMENT, *supra* note 2, at 53-54; *id.* 395 n.27.

[5] The Teller resolution made it clear that the United States would not annex Cuba. EXPANSIONISTS, *supra* note 2, at 230. It did not, however, bar the United States from seeking to annex the other former Spanish possessions (Puerto Rico, Guam, and the Philippines), and cession of these three territories to the United States was demanded by the American peace commissioners at the Paris peace conference. S. DOC. No. 62, 55th Cong., 3d Sess. (1899); W. REID, MAKING PEACE WITH SPAIN 40, 50-53, 150-58, 220 n.7 (1965) (edited version of the diary kept by Whitelaw Reid during the Paris peace conference of 1898). Spain acquiesced in these demands in the Treaty of Paris. Treaty of Paris, *supra* note 1, arts. II-III.

The reaction to American occupation in each of the three formerly Spanish insular territories foreshadowed each people's receptiveness to American rule and doubtlessly shaped the history and character of colonial administration in each of the territories. Although not as well known at first, the Filipinos' aspirations for independence were no less firm than those of the Cubans. On the day before the Senate voted on the Treaty of Paris,

> the drama of the decision was complicated and intensified by the arrival of news that the Filipinos had taken up arms in open revolt against the United States. There could be no more doubt of their desire for freedom

America's new role in world affairs: an abiding sense of mission and

or that the United States was now in the same position formerly occupied by discredited Spain.

C. WOODWARD, *supra* note 2, at 534.
The military occupation of the entire Filipino archipelago, ordered by President McKinley on December 21, 1898, had

> served to touch off a Filipino insurrection . . . . The insurrection, led by Emilio Auginaldo, lasted three sordid years and cost more than the war with Spain itself. Before it was put down, American forces had to resort to the same concentration-camp method that the Spanish had used to combat the guerrillas in Cuba. Thus a movement that had started as an effort to liberate the Cubans [the Spanish-American War] ended in a drive to subjugate the Filipinos.

2 R. HOFSTADTER, W. MILLER & D. AARON, THE AMERICAN REPUBLIC 340 (1959). As historian Julius W. Pratt has noted, "In annexing an empire, the United States had also annexed a war that was to prove much longer and more troublesome than that with Spain." COLONIAL EXPERIMENT, *supra* note 2, at 74. (For accounts of this brutal war, see R. DUPUY & W. BAUMER, THE LITTLE WARS OF THE UNITED STATES 65-99 (1968); Latane, *America as a World Power* 82-99, in 25 THE AMERICAN NATION: A HISTORY (A.B. Hart ed. 1907). For Filipino views on the Filipino-American War that followed the Spanish-American War, see J. ARCILLA, AN INTRODUCTION TO PHILIPPINE HISTORY 110-12 (1971); G. ZAIDE, REPUBLIC OF THE PHILIPPINES 204-12 (2d ed. 1970). This lengthy war and intense Filipino nationalism, *see* J. ARCILLA, *supra*, at 81-129; U. MAHAJANI, PHILIPPINE NATIONAL-ISM (1971); G. ZAIDE, *supra*, at 161-222, convinced President Woodrow Wilson that the Philippines were destined to become independent. In his annual address to Congress in 1913, President Wilson stated that the United States "must hold steadily in view [the Filipinos'] ultimate independence, and we must move toward the time of that independence as steadily as the way can be cleared and the foundations thoughtfully and permanently laid." 51 CONG. REC. 74, 75 (1913) (President's message). Congress declared its intention eventually to grant independence to the Philippines in 1916. *See* Jones Act (Philippines Islands), ch. 416, 39 Stat. 545 (1916) (preamble). Filipino independence was recognized in 1946 by Proc. No. 2695, 3 C.F.R. 86 (1946), *reprinted in* 22 U.S.C. § 1394 (1976).

In marked contrast, Guam and Puerto Rico generally welcomed the occupying forces and, for a considerable time, did not resist American rule. P. CARANO & P. SANCHEZ, A COMPLETE HISTORY OF GUAM 169-221 (1964) (Guam); M. GOLDING, A SHORT HISTORY OF PUERTO RICO 95 (1973); G. LEWIS, PUERTO RICO: FREEDOM AND POWER IN THE CARIBBEAN 103-04 (1963).

In 1898, Puerto Rico, the smaller Spanish colony in the Caribbean, had a less developed sense of nationhood than Cuba. Throughout the latter part of the nineteenth century, however, many Puerto Rican nationalists collaborated with Cubans in the struggle to liberate their respective islands from Spanish colonial rule. Among these nationalists were some of the most illustrious figures in Cuban and Puerto Rican history—men such as José Martí, Ramón Emeterio Betances and Eugenio María de Hostos. An anecdote illustrates their commitment to one another's cause: "When the Puerto Rican poet Pachín Marín joined the Cuban Revolutionary Party, José Martí asked him whether he was Cuban. 'Yes, sir,' said Marín. 'From which province?' asked Martí. 'From the province of Puerto Rico,' replied Marín." J. MARTÍ, MARTÍ Y PUERTO RICO 9-10 (1970 ed.) (author's translation). *See* R. BETANCES, LAS ANTILLAS PARA LOS ANTILLANOS (1975 ed.). Despite this common struggle for freedom from Spain, Puerto Rico's creole elite was less aggressive and demanding than its Cuban counterpart. While Cuban nationalists waged war for years against Spanish colonialism, the Puerto Rican political leadership had negotiated a form of local self-government or "autonomy" under an autonomic charter granted in 1897 by the Spanish *Cortes*. CONSTITUTION ESTABLISHING SELF-GOVERNMENT IN THE ISLAND OF PUERTO RICO BY SPAIN IN 1897, *reprinted in* OFFICE OF THE COMMONWEALTH OF PUERTO RICO, DOCUMENTS ON THE CONSTITUTIONAL HISTORY OF PUERTO RICO (1964) [hereinafter cited as CONSTITUTIONAL HISTORY OF

a certain nobility of purpose; a belief in the superiority of American institutions and values; an insensitivity or indifference to peoples and values imperfectly understood; and an ambivalence about the exercise of power combined with a deeply rooted innocence.[6]

The expansion of American power and influence precipitated a great national debate on imperialism, a debate that moved the nation for several years before and after the Spanish-American War and dominated the presidential election campaign of 1900.[7] The electoral victory of President William McKinley settled the controversy in favor of imperial expansion,[8] but the issue that remained was whether racially and culturally distinct peoples brought under American sovereignty without the promise of citizenship or statehood could be held indefinitely without doing violence to American values—that is, whether certain peoples could be permanently excluded from the American political community and deprived of equal rights.[9] Congress succeeded in resolving the citizenship question only after several years of debate. Ultimately, the two main territories were treated differently: the Jones Act of 1916 [10] promised

---

PUERTO RICO]. This constitution or autonomic charter was granted to the people of Puerto Rico to counter the "separatist feelings [that] were stirred in Puerto Rico" as a result of the Cuban war of independence. K. WAGENHEIM, PUERTO RICO: A PROFILE 61 (1970). It was negotiated by Luis Muñoz Rivera on the Puerto Rican side and Práxedes Sagasta on the Spanish side. Gordon Lewis has characterized Muñoz Rivera's middle-of-the-road policy as "opportunism dressed up as a wise empiricism." G. LEWIS, *supra*, at 64. Although this experiment with political autonomy was aborted by the American invasion of July 25, 1898, Puerto Rico's leaders generally held high hopes for achieving substantial self-government under the American flag. *See, e.g.,* 1 ANTOLOGÍA DEL PENSAMIENTO PUERTORRIQUEÑO 3-70 (E. Fernández Méndez ed. 1975) (collecting some of Luis Muñoz Rivera's writings); G. LEWIS, *supra*, at 103-04. Although American colonial administration soon disappointed many Puerto Ricans, *see, e.g.,* Muñoz Rivera, *El "Bill" Foraker*, in 1 ANTOLOGÍA DEL PENSAMIENTO PUERTORRIQUEÑO, *supra*, at 51-53, there was no resistance to American rule in Puerto Rico that is even remotely comparable to the open warfare and persistent nationalist agitation that arose in the Philippines.

[6] *See generally* COLONIAL EXPERIMENT, *supra* note 2.

[7] *See* UNITED STATES FOREIGN POLICY, *supra* note 2, at 219-21. *But see* Bailey, *Was the Presidential Election of 1900 a Mandate on Imperialism?*, 24 MISS. VALLEY HIST. REV. 43 (1937).

[8] *See generally* LaFeber, *Election of 1900*, in 3 HISTORY OF AMERICAN PRESIDENTIAL ELECTIONS 1789-1968, at 1877 (A. Schlesinger ed. 1971). Although "[t]he election of 1900 was not so much a ratification of colonialism as a repudiation of William Jennings Bryan," L. Gould, The Foraker Act: The Roots of American Colonial Policy 202 (1958) (unpublished thesis in the University of Michigan library), it nevertheless diminished the importance of the issue of imperialism for the American people. As a result of McKinley's victory, the expansionists were now relatively free to pursue their goals in Puerto Rico and the Philippines. For useful discussions of the significance of the issue of imperialism in the election of 1900, see *id.* 190-202; Bailey, *supra* note 7, at 43.

[9] *See* note 5 *supra*.

[10] Jones Act (Philippine Islands), ch. 416, 39 Stat. 545 (1916) (preamble declares intention of United States to recognize the independence of the Philippine

eventual independence to the Filipinos, but the Jones Act of 1917 [11] conferred American citizenship on the Puerto Ricans.

The collective naturalization of the Puerto Ricans one year after the Filipinos were promised their independence was a watershed in American colonial history and quite probably the turning point in Puerto Rico's political development. Having agreed in 1916 to grant independence to the larger and more intractable of the new insular territories, it is significant that Congress then chose to assert the permanence of the existing relationship with the smaller and more "loyal" territory.

Conferring United States citizenship [12] on the Puerto Ricans, however, did not alter the island's status as an American colony.

Islands). Filipino independence was recognized in 1946 by Proc. No. 2695, 3 C.F.R. 86 (1946), *reprinted in* 22 U.S.C. § 1394 (1976). On Guam, see note 460 *infra.*

[11] Jones Act (Puerto Rico), ch. 145, § 5, 39 Stat. 951 (1917) (current version at 8 U.S.C. § 1402 (1976)).

[12] The content of the concept of national citizenship under American law had been, and continues to be, less than definite or clear. *See generally* L. GETTYS, THE LAW OF CITIZENSHIP IN THE UNITED STATES (1934); F. VAN DYNE, CITIZENSHIP OF THE UNITED STATES (1904); Bickel, *Citizenship in the American Constitution*, 15 ARIZ. L. REV. 369 (1973). Citizenship had not been defined in the original Constitution and, as the late Professor Alexander M. Bickel reminded us, that Constitution "presented the edifying picture of a government that bestowed rights on people and persons, and held itself out as bound by certain standards of conduct in its relations with people and persons, not with some legal construct called citizen." A. BICKEL, THE MORALITY OF CONSENT 36 (1975). The notion of citizenship as the source of rights emerged in the *Dred Scott Case*, Scott v. Sanford, 60 U.S. (19 How.) 393 (1857), in which the Supreme Court held that rights and privileges under the Constitution were accorded to *citizens*, that citizenship and membership in the political community were synonymous, and that the concept of citizenship could not include "a negro of African descent, whose ancestors were of pure African blood, and who were brought to this country and sold as slaves." *Id.* 400-05. The baleful results of the decision in the *Dred Scott Case* had been effectively overruled in the Civil Rights Act of 1866, ch. 31, § 1, 14 Stat. 27 ("all persons born in the United States and not subject to any foreign power, excluding Indians not taxed, are hereby declared to be citizens of the United States") and by the fourteenth amendment to the Constitution, U.S. CONST. amend. XIV, § 1 ("[a]ll persons born or naturalized in the United States, and subject to the jurisdiction thereof, are citizens of the United States and of the State in which they reside"). However, as Professor Bickel observed, in the process Congress revived the concept of citizenship. A. BICKEL, *supra*, at 40. As a result, despite a "tradition of denuding the concept of citizenship in our law of any special role and content," our courts and our political leaders have not infrequently "returned to a rhetoric of exalting citizenship which echoes the Taney opinion in *Dred Scott.*" *Id.* 50. *See also* cases cited at *id.* 51-52 nn.35-38.

At the turn of the century, the exaltation of American citizenship—by imperialist and anti-imperialist alike—was a notable and not surprising characteristic of the expansive and optimistic period during which the United States embarked upon its colonial enterprise. If the imprecisely defined concept of citizenship involved more than the rights to go to the seat of government, to invoke the protection of the national government when abroad, to use the navigable waters of the United States, and to bring an action in a Federal court (under diversity jurisdiction), A. BICKEL, *supra*, at 44; Coudert, *Our New Peoples: Citizens, Subjects, Nationals or Aliens*, 3 COLUM. L. REV. 13 (1903), it surely was the sense of permanent inclusion in the American political community in a non-subordinate condition, in contrast to the

By bestowing citizenship upon the inhabitants of the island, Congress proclaimed the future of Puerto Rico to be something other than national independence and thereby sought to resolve the question how the United States would deal with this part of its empire. Accordingly, the citizenship granted was not complete; it was never intended to confer on the Puerto Ricans "any rights that the American people [did] not want them to have." [13] The very word "citizenship" suggested equality of rights and privileges and full membership in the American political community, thereby obscuring the colonial relationship between a great metropolitan state and a poor

---

position of aliens, subjects or even nationals. Dred Scott had been held not to fall within the term "people of the United States," though he was clearly a *subject* of the United States—that is, a person owing allegiance to the United States and not to any other nation. The Civil Rights Act of 1866 and the fourteenth amendment had abolished the distinction between citizen and subject as far as black persons were concerned. However, the forcible annexation of formerly Spanish insular territories once again created a class of persons who clearly owed allegiance to the United States (as a result of the transfer of sovereignty) but who arguably were not citizens of the United States. The term *national*, often used interchangeably with the word *citizen* when referring to (or defining) the status of an individual in relation to the state, evolved into a term broader in scope than citizen. "The term *citizen*, in its general acceptation, is applicable only to a person who is endowed with full political and civil rights in the body politic of the state." 3 G. HACKWORTH, DIGEST OF INTERNATIONAL LAW 1 (1942). National, on the other hand, includes "a person who, though not a citizen, owes permanent allegiance to the state and is entitled to its protection." *Id.* 1-2. Based on this distinction, although all citizens are nationals, all nationals are not citizens. Coudert, *supra.* The legal construct of national served the nation's imperial purposes; the most notable examples of persons who were nationals of the United States though not citizens (in the absence of positive action by Congress) were the native peoples of the new colonial possessions of the United States.

The Foraker Act granted the inhabitants of Puerto Rico the status of United States nationals. It provided, *inter alia*, that

> all inhabitants continuing to reside [in Puerto Rico] . . . who were Spanish subjects on the eleventh day of April, eighteen hundred and ninety-nine and then resided in Porto Rico, and their children born subsequent thereto, shall be deemed and held to be *citizens of Porto Rico*, and as such entitled to the protection of the United States, except such as shall have elected to preserve their allegiance to the Crown of Spain.

Foraker Act (Puerto Rico) ch. 191, § 7, 31 STAT. 77 (1900) (emphasis added). Although these "citizens of Porto Rico" were not citizens of the United States, they were nevertheless not aliens, and they were expected to transfer their allegiance from Spain to the United States and receive in return the protection of the United States. The status of national, as distinguished from citizen, became a convenient construct for those who favored territorial expansion but did not wish to make the people of the new territory citizens of the United States or otherwise suggest that they might aspire to equality under the American constitutional system. *See* Gonzales v. Williams, 192 U.S. 1, 12-13 (1904). Under the Act of June 14, 1902, ch. 1088, 32 Stat. 386 (1902), United States passports could be issued to "persons . . . owing allegiance, *whether citizens or not*, to the United States," *id.* (emphasis supplied), including, of course, Puerto Ricans. *See* note 460 *infra.*

[13] 33 CONG. REC. 2473 (1900) (remarks of Sen. Foraker). *See* text accompanying note 139 *infra.*

overseas dependency.   But the creation of a second-class citizenship for a community of persons that was given no expectation of equality under the American system had the effect of perpetuating the colonial status of Puerto Rico.

Puerto Rico's anomalous status later made it possible to devise an unusual series of relationships with the United States.   In 1950 Congress enacted legislation permitting the establishment of the Commonwealth of Puerto Rico.[14]   Although Puerto Ricans remained effectively disenfranchised with respect to the federal government and had no vote in the election of the United States President, this new political arrangement gave them greater control of their internal government and the opportunity to draft a Puerto Rican constitution.[15]   Before and after the establishment of the Commonwealth of Puerto Rico, Congress extended to the island's people various federal statutory benefits while exempting them from other types of legislation, including some on federal income taxation.[16]   Given a voice in determining their island's political future, Puerto Rican voters have chosen to retain commonwealth status rather than support processes culminating either in statehood or independence.[17]   But in 1968 a pro-statehood governor was elected,[18] and in 1976 the statehood movement for the first time won every major elective political office.[19]   In recent years, however, the pro-independence minority has become increasingly active as well and

---

[14] Pub. L. No. 81-600, 64 Stat. 319 (1950) (codified at 48 U.S.C. §§ 731-916 (1976)).

[15] 48 U.S.C. §§ 731b-731c (1976).

[16] I.R.C. § 933.   This specific exemption is necessary because § 9 of the Puerto Rico Federal Relations Act, Pub. L. No. 81-600, 64 Stat. 319 (codified at 48 U.S.C. § 734 (1976)), provides that "[t]he statutory laws of the United States not locally inapplicable shall have the same force and effect in Puerto Rico as in the United States."

[17] In a 1967 plebiscite on political status, 60.41% of the voters supported a reformed or "perfected" form of commonwealth status, and 38.98% favored statehood. Independence advocates boycotted the plebiscite; the independence option received 0.6% of the vote, AD HOC ADVISORY GROUP ON THE PRESIDENTIAL VOTE FOR PUERTO RICO, THE PRESIDENTIAL VOTE FOR PUERTO RICO 4 (1971); *Puerto Rico Vote Strongly Favors a Commonwealth*, N.Y. Times, July 24, 1967, at 1, col. 1.

[18] *Puerto Rico Race Is Won by Ferré*, N.Y. Times, Nov. 7, 1968, at 9, col. 1.

[19] *See* note 28 & 29 *infra* & accompanying text.   The current governor of Puerto Rico, Carlos Romero Barceló, finds that in 1917 an "implied pledge of statehood [was] made to Puerto Ricans when citizenship was granted."   Address by Governor Carlos Romero Barceló, before Los Angeles World Affairs Council (Dec. 6, 1977) (copy on file at the *University of Pennsylvania Law Review*).   *See* Cabranes, *Puerto Rico: Out of the Colonial Closet*, 33 FOREIGN POL'Y 66 (Winter 1978-79).

has repeatedly asked the United Nations to declare Puerto Rico a "non-self-governing territory" under the United Nations Charter.[20] In 1978, the leaders of all major Puerto Rican political parties for the first time appeared before the United Nations' Special Committee on Decolonization, which thereafter adopted a resolution critical of alleged United States violations of the Puerto Ricans' "national rights." [21] Eighty years after the acquisition of the island from Spain, Puerto Rico's relationship with the United States remains a controversial subject on both the national and international political agendas.[22]

---

[20] U.N. CHART. art. 73. On the activities of the pro-independence minority, see Berríos Martínez, Independence for Puerto Rico: The Only Solution, 55 FOREIGN AFFAIRS 561 (1977); Cabranes, The Status of Puerto Rico, 16 INT'L & COMP. L.Q. 531 (1967).

[21] See 33 U.N. GAOR, Special Committee on the Situation with Regard to the Implementation of the Declaration on the Granting of Independence to Colonial Countries and Peoples (1133d mtg.), U.N. Doc. A/AC.109/574 (1978); Cabranes, supra note 19; NEWSWEEK, Sept. 11, 1978, at 35. See also note 22 infra.

[22] As recently as June, 1976, the Supreme Court could drolly say that it does not "appear that the debate over the relationship of Puerto Rico to the United States has ended even now." Examining Bd. of Eng'rs, Architects & Surveyors v. Flores de Otero, 426 U.S. 572, 599 n.30 (1976).

On the persistence of the international and municipal debate on the status of Puerto Rico, see 1974 DIGEST OF UNITED STATES PRACTICE IN INTERNATIONAL LAW 51-52; 1975 DIGEST OF UNITED STATES PRACTICE IN INTERNATIONAL LAW 21, 24, 90-92; 1976 DIGEST OF UNITED STATES PRACTICE IN INTERNATIONAL LAW 51-53; Cabranes, The Applicability of the Principle of Self-determination to Unintegrated Territories of the United States: The Cases of Puerto Rico and The Trust Territory of the Pacific Islands, 67 AM. SOC'Y INT'L L. PROC. 1 (1973); Cabranes, supra note 20.

The subject of Puerto Rico's status has been before the United Nations General Assembly, in one form or another, since the organization's founding. In 1953 the United States succeeded in having Puerto Rico removed from the United Nations' list of non-self-governing territories. G.A. Res. 748 (VIII), 8 U.N. GAOR, Supp. (No. 17) 25, U.N. Doc. A/2630 (1953); CASES ON UNITED NATIONS LAW 791-804 (L. Sohn ed. 1956). In recent years, however, Cuba and other third world countries have attempted to restore Puerto Rico to this list, which has aroused the interest of international lawyers and commentators on international relations. See, e.g., Note, Puerto Rico: Colony or Commonwealth?, 6 N.Y.U. J. INT'L L. & POL. 115 (1953); Hypocrisy at the U.N., N.Y. Times, Sept. 2, 1976, at 30, col. 1 (editorial); Reason on Puerto Rico, N.Y. Times, Sept. 9, 1976, at 38, col. 2 (editorial); N.Y. Times, Sept. 22, 1976, at 40, col. 3 (letter of A. F. Lowenthal). See also 33 U.N. GAOR, Special Committee on the Situation with Regard to the Implementation of the Declaration on the Granting of Independence to Colonial Countries and Peoples (1133d mtg.), U.N. Doc. A/AC.109/574 (1978); Cabranes, supra note 19.

The island's so-called "commonwealth" status has drawn no visible support from the developing world; conferences of nonaligned states repeatedly have urged independence for the island. A recent third world call for independence for Puerto Rico came at the conference of nonaligned leaders held in August, 1976, in Colombo, Sri Lanka. Nonaligned End Meeting With Warning to the Rich, N.Y. Times, Aug. 20, 1976, § A, at 3, col. 1.

For the past two decades, proponents of the island's commonwealth status have unsuccessfully tried to reform the island's relationship with the United States. See Puerto Rico—1963: Hearings on H.R. 5945, H.R. 5946, H.R. 5947, H.R. 5948, H.R. 5991, H.R. 6047, H.R. 6076, and H.R. 6083, Before the Subcomm. on Territorial

The story of how and why Puerto Ricans became American citizens is not, therefore, without contemporary significance, nor is it of interest only to Puerto Ricans. Quite apart from the persistent debate on Puerto Rico's political relationship to the United States, American citizenship has vitally affected the place of Puerto Ricans in the American political system and economy. American citizenship made possible the mass migration of Puerto Ricans to the North American continent in the years following the Second World War [23] and today affects the character of the political and constitutional claims asserted in the continental United States by Puerto Ricans.[24] Moreover, the growing demands of Puerto Rico

---

and Insular Affairs of the House Comm. on Interior and Insular Affairs, 88th Cong., 1st Sess. (1963); *Hearings on S. 2023 Before the Senate Comm. on Interior and Insular Affairs,* 86th Cong., 1st Sess. (1959); *Hearings on H.R. 9234 Before a Special Subcomm. on Territorial and Insular Affairs of the House Comm. on Interior and Insular Affairs,* 86th Cong., 1st Sess. (1959); AD HOC ADVISORY GROUP ON PUERTO RICO, COMPACT OF PERMANENT UNION BETWEEN PUERTO RICO AND THE UNITED STATES (1975); UNITED STATES-PUERTO RICO COMMISSION ON THE STATUS OF PUERTO RICO, STATUS OF PUERTO RICO: REPORT OF THE UNITED STATES COMMISSION ON THE STATUS OF PUERTO RICO (1966). Two bills related to the proposed compact were introduced in Congress in 1975 but died. H.R. 11200, 94th Cong., 1st Sess., 121 CONG. REC. 41487 (1975); S.J. Res. 215, 94th Cong., 2d Sess., 122 CONG. REC. S. 16383 (daily ed. Sept. 22, 1976).

On the growing movement to make Puerto Rico a state of the American union, see notes 28-32 *infra.*

[23] *See generally* C. SENIOR, STRANGERS—THEN NEIGHBORS: FROM PILGRIMS TO PUERTO RICANS (1961). American legislators did not anticipate that extending citizenship to the inhabitants of Puerto Rico would lead to the substantial northward migration of the forties and fifties. Max Lerner, commenting upon American legislative attempts to prevent "undesirable" racial and ethnic groups from entering the country, writes: "The irony of the exclusionist policy was that since it could not be applied to Puerto Rico (which was part of territorial America) the exclusionists had to tolerate the [post-World War Two] influx of Puerto Ricans . . . ." M. LERNER, AMERICA AS A CIVILIZATION 92 (1957). In 1976, the United States Commission on Civil Rights noted:

> The Puerto Rican migration to the mainland has been unique. It is the only massive migratory movement to the United States mainland of American citizens. These Americans are generally distinct in language and culture and have different customs. . . .
>
> . . . . .
>
> The United States has never before had a large migration of citizens from offshore, distinct in culture and language and also facing the problem of color prejudice.

U.S. COMMISSION ON CIVIL RIGHTS, PUERTO RICANS IN THE CONTINENTAL UNITED STATES: AN UNCERTAIN FUTURE 144-45 (1976). For the Commission's catalogue of claims on behalf of these citizens, see *id.* 146-52.

[24] Several such claims have been asserted with notable success and adopted in federal legislation. One example is the prohibition of the enforcement against persons educated in Puerto Rico of state laws requiring English literacy. *See, e.g.,* Katzenbach v. Morgan, 384 U.S. 641 (1966) (upholding § 4(e) of the Voting Rights Act of 1965, Pub. L. No. 89-110, § 4(e), 79 Stat. 437, and outlawing New York's requirement of literacy in English as a prerequisite to voting as applied to persons educated in Puerto Rico); Torres v. Sachs, 381 F. Supp. 309 (S.D.N.Y. 1974) (finding that

on the federal treasury—$3,026,420,000 in federal "outlays" in fiscal year 1976,[25] including approximately $593,000,000 in food stamps alone [26]—are clearly rooted in the American citizenship granted in 1917. So, too, is the proposal to grant United States citizens residing in Puerto Rico the right to vote for President and Vice President of the United States—a proposal vigorously endorsed in 1971 by a joint commission appointed by the President of the United States and the Governor of Puerto Rico.[27] Perhaps the most important by-product of the grant of citizenship is the strong and growing political movement to make Puerto Rico a state of the American Union.[28] The movement's sweeping electoral success in

---

New York City's practice of conducting its elections exclusively in English deprived the plaintiff of the right to vote, and ordering New York City election officials to disseminate election information in both English and Spanish and to provide voters with bilingual ballots). Another example is the promotion of Spanish language or bilingual educational programs in American cities with substantial Spanish speaking populations. The Bilingual Education Act, 20 U.S.C. §§ 880b to 880b-5 (1976) is an example of recent governmental efforts to address the needs of children whose first language is not English. This Act

> declares it to be the policy of the United States to provide financial assistance to local educational agencies to develop and carry out new and imaginative elementary and secondary school programs designed to meet [the] . . . special educational needs . . . [of] children who come from environments where the dominant language is other than English.

Id. § 880b.

Additionally, demands that Spanish be accorded some form of official recognition —even parity with English—in voting procedures and official ballots are increasingly common in communities with substantial Puerto Rican populations.

[25] Letter to the author from Michael E. Veve, Deputy Administrator, Office of the Commonwealth of Puerto Rico, Washington, D.C. (October 31, 1978) (copy on file at the *University of Pennsylvania Law Review*). *See also Benitez: Achievements in D.C. "Good, Pleasing,"* San Juan Star, Oct. 1, 1976, at 3; Dorvillier, *What Has Jaime Wrought?*, San Juan Star, Oct. 3, 1976, at 6.

[26] Letter from Michael E. Veve, *supra* note 25; Letter from Mrs. Sara Ehrman, Special Assistant, Office of the Commonwealth of Puerto Rico, to author (Nov. 30, 1976) (copy on file at the *University of Pennsylvania Law Review*). At hearings concerning the food stamp program, former Resident Commissioner Jaime Benitez defended the administration of the program in Puerto Rico, despite what some American legislators consider to be its disproportionately high costs, and advocated "the full extension of the program to *fellow citizens* on the island." *Food Stamp Reform: Hearings on S. 1993, S. 2369, S. 2451, and S. 2537 Before the Subcomm. on Agric. Research and Gen. Legislation of the Sen. Comm. on Agric. and Forestry,* 94th Cong., 1st Sess., pt. 2, at 752 (1975) (statement of Resident Comm'r Jaime Benítez) (emphasis added).

[27] AD HOC ADVISORY GROUP ON THE PRESIDENTIAL VOTE FOR PUERTO RICO, *supra* note 17.

[28] In the general election of 1952, the first such election held after the establishment of the Commonwealth of Puerto Rico, the party favoring statehood for the island received 12.9% of the vote. In the same election, the Puerto Rican Independence Party won 18.9% of the vote, and the party favoring the new commonwealth status—the Popular Democratic Party—won 67.0%.

Puerto Rico in 1976 [29] was reinforced by President Ford's espousal of the idea in the last days of his presidency [30] and President Carter's expressed readiness to support Puerto Rican statehood if the island's people formally request it.[31]

The results of subsequent quadrennial elections show a significant growth in the statehood movement, at the expense of those parties favoring independence or continued commonwealth status. The results of these elections are shown below.

	Part(y)(ies) Favoring Statehood	Part(y)(ies) Favoring Commonwealth	Part(y)(ies) Favoring Independence
1956	25.0%	62.5%	12.5%
1960	32.1%	58.2%	3.1%
1964	34.7%	59.4%	2.7%
1968	45.1%	52.1%	2.8%
1972	44.0%	51.4%	4.5%
1976	48.3%	45.3%	6.4%

Letter to author from Michael E. Veve, Deputy Administrator, Office of the Commonwealth of Puerto Rico, Washington, D.C. (October 27, 1978) (copy in author's files) (copy on file at *University of Pennsylvania Law Review*). The figures shown reflect only those parties favoring a particular status alternative. Because of the exclusion of those political parties not representing or advocating a particular status, the sum of the percentages for any given year may not equal 100%. In 1968, a split of the pro-commonwealth forces into two parties—one receiving 42% of the vote and the other 10%—resulted in the election of the first pro-statehood governor, Luis A. Ferré. In 1972, a reunited Popular Democratic Party regained the governorship, but by the smallest margin in three decades. Office of the Commonwealth of Puerto Rico, Puerto Rico: Basic Political, Social and Economic Data 8 (Washington, D.C., Feb. 1976) [hereinafter cited as Basic Data] (copy on file at *University of Pennsylvania Law Review*). In 1976, the pro-statehood New Progressive Party won the governorship, most important mayoralties, and control of both houses of the Puerto Rico legislature. *See* notes 29 & 30 *infra*. The pro-independence vote in 1976 was split between the democratic socialist Puerto Rican Independence Party (5.70%) and the Marxist-Leninist Puerto Rican Socialist Party (.74%). Letter to author from Michael E. Veve, Director, Legal Counsel Section, Office of the Commonwealth of Puerto Rico, Washington, D.C. (March 28, 1978) (copy on file at *University of Pennsylvania Law Review*). For the first time, the combined vote of the anti-commonwealth parties—the parties united in the belief that commonwealth status is a colonial form of government that ought to be ended—exceeded that of the pro-commonwealth forces. Indeed, the combined vote of the pro-statehood and pro-independence parties constituted, for the first time, a substantial majority of the Puerto Rican electorate. Basic Data, *supra*, at 8. The current governor of Puerto Rico, Carlos Romero Barceló, has stated that he will hold a plebiscite on the statehood question if he is re-elected in 1980. NEWSWEEK, Sept. 11, 1978, at 35. *See* President's Statement on 26th Anniversary of the Commonwealth of Puerto Rico (July 25, 1978), 14 WEEKLY COMP. OF PRES. DOC. 1336 (July 31, 1978) [hereinafter referred to as President's Statement] ("[T]he United States remains fully committed to the principle of self-determination for the people of Puerto Rico.").

[29] *Pro-Statehood Candidate Stages Puerto Rican Upset*, N.Y. Times, Nov. 3, 1976, at 1, col. 4.

[30] *President Proposes Puerto Rican State; Urges U.S. Initiative*, N.Y. Times, Jan. 1, 1977, at 1, col. 6; Vidal, *A Change in Posture: Ford Statement Marks the First Time a President Has Appealed for Statehood for Puerto Rico*, N.Y. Times, Jan. 1, 1977, at 1, col. 4. President Ford's message to the Congress on Puerto Rican statehood was sent on January 14, 1977. N.Y. Times, Jan. 15, 1977, at 22, col. 1.

[31] Mr. Carter, then president-elect, responded to President Ford's statement on Puerto Rico by saying, *inter alia*, that "I would be perfectly willing to see Puerto

In short, many of the difficult international and domestic policy questions raised by an initiative for formal integration of Puerto Rico into the American union have their roots in the collective naturalization of the Puerto Ricans in 1917 and the creation of a class whose rights and privileges under the Constitution were regarded as inferior to those of fellow citizens in the continental United States.[32]   In the first two decades of this century, American policymakers took it for granted that Puerto Rico would permanently remain an American colony, and the Supreme Court found colonialism constitutionally tolerable.   Indifferent or hostile to the idea of eventual equality for the Puerto Ricans through statehood, and unaware of any clear-cut or vigorous demand for an independent Puerto Rico, the United States government extended American citizenship to the Puerto Ricans as a token of the permanence of the island's political relationship to the United States.   Puerto Rico and the United States will undoubtedly continue to be deeply affected by that legislation.

Despite Congress' pivotal role in Puerto Rico's history and in shaping United States policy toward its dependencies, there is no published account of the origins and development in Congress of the idea of making Puerto Ricans citizens of the United States.   In Puerto Rico, two versions of popular history have coexisted for more than half a century.   A substantial body of opinion in Puerto Rico would agree with Chief Justice Taft that between 1898 and

Rico become a state if the people who live there prefer that." *Carter Weighing Personnel to Fill Sub-cabinet Jobs; Disagrees with Ford on Puerto Rican State,* N.Y. Times, Jan. 2, 1977, at 1, col. 5; *id.* 44, col. 5.   Both statements were unprecedented.   Mayor Maurice A. Ferré of Miami, an avowed proponent of Puerto Rican statehood, read a message from Mr. Carter to the people of Puerto Rico at the inauguration of pro-statehood Governor Carlos Romero Barceló.   The message referred to the 1976 Democratic Party platform's endorsement of either commonwealth status or statehood depending on the wishes of the people of Puerto Rico, and added: "My Party's Platform, on which I ran for the Presidency, clearly states the recognition of Puerto Rico's right to political self-determination.   I fully subscribe to and support this expressed right, whatever your choice may be."   San Juan Star, Jan. 5, 1977, at 16.   *See also The Commonwealth of Puerto Rico,* The Washington Post, Jan. 4, 1977, § A, at 12, col. 1 (editorial); President's Statement, *supra* note 28.

[32] President-elect Carter's statement to the people of Puerto Rico noted that "[t]he Constitution of the United States does not distinguish between citizens.   We do not have in our country first and second class citizens."   San Juan Star, Jan. 5, 1977, at 16.   David Vidal, writing in *The New York Times,* notes that "[t]he granting of citizenship in 1917 on United States initiative did not change the status debate, but to some it made statehood logical and inevitable.   To this day, that is a prime argument offered in favor of statehood."   *Puerto Ricans Disagree Sharply Over the Advantages of Statehood,* N.Y. Times, Jan. 9, 1977, at 1, col. 2; *id.* 44, col. 3.   For an explanation of why and how the citizenship held by Puerto Ricans differs from that of United States citizens residing in the continental United States, see Balzac v. Porto Rico, 258 U.S. 298 (1922).

1917 "[i]t became a yearning of the Porto Ricans to be American
Citizens . . . and [the Jones Act of 1917] gave them the boon." [33]
The other version of popular history, which seems to enjoy greater
prominence in the literature and lore on the subject, claims that
United States citizenship was imposed upon the Puerto Ricans. It
is frequently suggested that the grant of citizenship was dictated by
strategic necessities of World War I or by the desire to enlist Puerto
Rican youths into the United States armed forces.[34] Leaders of the
island's independence movement and others have alleged that "reasons of war" dictated the congressional decision to confer United
States citizenship on the Puerto Ricans.[35] In Puerto Rico there is

---

[33] Balzac v. Porto Rico, 258 U.S. at 308. Felix Frankfurter, serving in 1914
as Law Officer of the Bureau of Insular Affairs of the Department of War, saw the
grant of American citizenship "as a means of removing the great source of political
unrest in the Island." F. Frankfurter, The Political Status of Porto Rico 7 (March
11, 1914) (memorandum of law to Secretary of War in archives of the United
States) (copy on file at the *University of Pennsylvania Law Review*). For typical
expressions of views similar to those of Taft and Frankfurter in the contemporary
Puerto Rican press, see Guerra, *En Torno a la Fortaleza*, El Mundo, April 17, 1974,
§ A, at 6, col. 6; Vázquez, *Hace 58 años*, El Nuevo Día, March 1, 1975, at 22.

The literature claiming that American citizenship was extended to the people
of Puerto Rico as a result of Puerto Rican demands or yearnings is, understandably,
associated with proponents of one or another form of permanent union of the
island with the United States through statehood or continued commonwealth status.
In this literature, there is a tendency to describe citizenship as having been
"granted" or "conferred" (*concedido*) in 1917 by Congress, terms which suggest a
response by Congress to expressions of Puerto Rican aspirations or longings. *See*,
e.g., J. CÓRDOVA, CITIZENSHIP 1, 10 (1971) (Office of the Commonwealth of Puerto
Rico, Washington, D.C., Puerto Rico Booklets Series No. 7, 1971) (copy on file at
the *University of Pennsylvania Law Review*); Vásquez, *supra*.

[34] Although the view that American citizenship was "imposed" upon Puerto
Ricans has much support among proponents of national independence for the island,
it is also supported by some public figures in Puerto Rico not associated with the
independence movement. *See*, *e.g.*, García Passalacqua, *The Puerto Ricans*, N.Y.
Times, Oct. 7, 1973, § 7 (Book Review), at 24 ("[T]he Puerto Ricans were made
American citizens by a unilateral act of Congress dictated by the strategic necessities
of World War I."). For a typical viewpoint of advocates of independence, see
M. MALDONADO-DENIS, PUERTO RICO: A SOCIO-HISTORIC INTERPRETATION 108
(1972) ("The Jones Act imposed North American citizenship collectively on the
Puerto Rican people. And from that very instant the road was open for the
recruitment of Puerto Rican youths into the United States armed forces."). *See also*
M. ARCE DE VÁZQUEZ, LA OBRA LITERARIA DE JOSÉ DE DIEGO 47 (1967).

[35] *See*, *e.g.*, M. MALDONADO-DENIS, *supra* note 34. The late Pedro Albizu
Campos, the long-time leader of the Nationalist Party of Puerto Rico, claimed that
"reasons of war" (*razones de guerra*) accounted for the extension of United States
citizenship to the Puerto Ricans. El Nacionalista de Puerto Rico, Nov. 15, 1930,
at 9, col. 1. *See also* P. ALBIZU CAMPOS, INDEPENDENCIA ECONÓMICA 34-35
(Publicaciones de Forún, Federación de Organizaciones Estudiantiles de la U.P.R.
1970). Professor R.W. Anderson seems to allude to this widely circulated notion
when he writes: "As United States citizens after 1917, Puerto Ricans were guaranteed free movement between the island and the mainland; *they were also subject
to compulsory military service,* a fact that was subsequently to have economic
importance in terms of veterans' benefits." R. ANDERSON, PARTY POLITICS IN
PUERTO RICO 14 (1965) (emphasis added). Although Professor Anderson does not

to this day a widely held belief, expressed in 1928 by a leading Puerto Rican writer, who later became attorney general, Vicente Géigel Polanco, that "[t]he 'conferral' of [United States] citizenship was not an act of justice, but rather, an imposition of the American government." [36]

These conflicting versions of the central event of Puerto Rico's twentieth century political history confirm the observation of the British historian Richard Pares that in colonial societies "[g]ood history cannot do so much service as money or science; but bad history can do almost as much harm as the most disastrous scientific discovery in the world." [37] Both versions assume that Puerto Rican opinion on the subject, as expressed by the island's leaders, was clearly articulated and readily understood in the executive and legislative branches of the American government. Both versions assume that the leading protagonists—the United States Congress and the island's leadership—acted with a full appreciation of the implications of the citizenship legislation. These assumptions are unwarranted. The Puerto Ricans neither yearned for United States citizenship nor did Congress intend to impose it upon them. As is often the case, the truth lies somewhere between contradictory historical theses.

The 1917 legislation extending United States citizenship to the people of Puerto Rico was adopted a month before the Congress resolved to recognize the existence of a state of war against Germany.[38] There is no evidence, however, that the timing of the two

---

explicitly state that military conscription was a factor that motivated Congress to extend United States citizenship to the Puerto Ricans, he clearly suggests that there is a direct link between citizenship and compulsory military service, and that the former was the predicate for the latter.

Nilita Vientós Gastón, a leading Puerto Rican intellectual and civic leader, shares this view: "'The Puerto Rican is an American citizen, but *what kind* of citizen? A citizen who doesn't enjoy all the rights or privileges. Why were we given that citizenship? Only to take us into wars, nothing else!'" H. YURCHENCO, ¡HABLAMOS! PUERTO RICANS SPEAK 119 (1971) (emphasis in original). *See also* L. CRIPPS, PUERTO RICO 23-24 (1974); K. WAGENHEIM, PUERTO RICO 69 (1970). *But see* M. GOLDING, A SHORT HISTORY OF PUERTO RICO 121-22 (1973).

[36] Géigel Polanco, *El Mito de la Ciudadanía*, El Mundo, Dec. 10, 1928, at 6, col. 3 (translation by the author).

[37] Pares, *The Revolt Against Colonialism*, in THE HISTORIAN'S BUSINESS 77, 82 (R. & E. Humphreys ed. 1961).

[38] On April 2, 1917, President Woodrow Wilson urged a special session of Congress to declare war on Germany. 55 CONG. REC. 102 (1917) (address of President Wilson). On April 4, the Senate passed a joint resolution recognizing the existence of a state of war with Germany. S.J. Res. 1, 65th Cong., 1st Sess., 55 CONG. REC. 261 (1917). One day later the House of Representatives followed suit. *Id.* 412-13. In March, Congress had extended American citizenship to the inhabitants of Puerto Rico. Jones Act (Puerto Rico), ch. 145, § 5, 39 Stat. 951 (1917) (current version at 8 U.S.C. § 1402 (1976)). That the Jones Act was

actions by Congress was anything but coincidental. The author is unaware of any evidence of a design by anyone in the American government during this period to make extensive use of Puerto Ricans in the armed services or to make Puerto Ricans citizens on the theory that they might then be conscripted. Indeed, the number of Puerto Ricans who served in the First World War appears to have been quite small, and much of that service was in the relative backwater of the Panama Canal Zone.[39] Moreover, the incorporation of a force of Puerto Rican soldiers into the United States Army long antedated the war; a Puerto Rican regiment was first organized in 1899.[40]

By extending United States citizenship to the Puerto Ricans after promising independence to the Filipinos, Congress intended to do little more than proclaim the permanence of Puerto Rico's political links with the United States. The apparent readiness of the Puerto Ricans to accept a continuing association with the United States—confirmed by the absence of sustained and systematic opposition to the proposal or significant resistance to colonial rule [41] like

---

adopted in early 1917 rather than during the previous summer, however, was the result of a crowded agenda. President Wilson had pressed for the new act since 1914. 4 A. LINK, WILSON: CONFUSIONS AND CRISES 1915-1916, at 356 n.141 (1964).

[39] The only Puerto Rican unit of any significance during World War I was the Puerto Rico Regiment of Infantry, which served in the Canal Zone from May 1917 through March 1919. 3 UNITED STATES ARMY WAR COLLEGE, HISTORICAL REVISION, ORDER OF BATTLE OF THE UNITED STATES LAND FORCES IN THE WORLD WAR (1917-19), pt. 2, at 1405 (1949) [hereinafter cited as ORDER OF BATTLE]. This unit was originally organized in 1899 as a provisional regiment. *Id.* In 1908, its two battalions were made part of the United States Army. An Act Fixing the Status of the Porto Rico Provisional Regiment of Infantry, ch. 201, 35 Stat. 392 (1908). Although a Puerto Rican division was contemplated during the war, it was never organized. Instead, the War Department ordered the organization of a provisional division. The men for this division were to come from the first Puerto Rican draft. On October 1, 1918, over 10,000 Puerto Rican officers and men were organized into the Provisional Tactical Brigade. Less than two months later, however, this unit was ordered disbanded. ORDER OF BATTLE, *supra*, at 661-62.

[40] *See* note 39 *supra.*

[41] Regarding the reception the Puerto Ricans accorded their American invaders, one observer has written: "In 1898, when the Americans landed in Puerto Rico, the islanders, who had by then developed into a distinct people with their own literature and art, and who had retained the warm friendly attitudes and sweet smiles of their earlier ancestors, . . . welcomed the invaders." L. CRIPPS, *supra* note 35, at 9-10. In part, at least, the lack of resistance displayed by the Puerto Ricans upon the transfer of sovereignty is accounted for by their expectation that the Americans would treat them benevolently. *Id.* 10. Some authors have concluded from this and other episodes that Puerto Ricans are a docile and passive people; others argue that the notion of the "docile Puerto Rican" is "a colonialist's construct based on a determinist concept." J. SILÉN, WE, THE PUERTO RICAN PEOPLE 45 (1971). *But see* R. MARQUÉS, THE DOCILE PUERTO RICAN (1976) (originally published in Spanish as EL PUERTORRIQUEÑO DÓCIL (1962)). The difficulties encountered by the United States in pacifying the Philippines are described in W. POMEROY, AMERICAN NEO-COLONIALISM 64-98 (1970).

that of the Filipinos [42]—seemed to validate the view that citizenship would amply fulfill the expectations of the Puerto Rican people.

In any event, American citizenship is not a prerequisite to conscription: aliens were made subject to the draft during the Civil War, the Spanish-American War and World War I.[43] The United States did not have to confer American citizenship on the people of Puerto Rico in order to be able to draft Puerto Rican men during World War I. These men would have been subject to conscription into military service even if they had remained "citizens of Puerto Rico." The natives of Puerto Rico had for years been considered nationals [44] of the United States—that is, they were non-citizens, although clearly not aliens, who owed allegiance to the United

---

[42] For an account of Filipino resistance to American rule, see J. BLOUNT, THE AMERICAN OCCUPATION OF THE PHILIPPINES 1898-1912, at 186-523 (1912). But at least one student of the conflict attributes American success in suppressing the Filipino insurgents to "[t]he American policy of benevolence and the many humanitarian acts of the Army" rather than military superiority. J. Gates, An Experiment in Benevolent Pacification 360 (May 25, 1967) (unpublished thesis in Duke University Library).

[43] Noncitizens under the jurisdiction of the United States first became subject to the draft during the Civil War. The Civil War Conscription Act of 1863 made "all able-bodied male citizens . . . , *and persons of foreign birth* who shall have declared on oath their intention to become citizens . . . liable to perform military duty in the service of the United States. . . ." Civil War Conscription Act, ch. 75, § 1, 12 Stat. 731 (1863) (emphasis added). This language was repeated (nearly word for word) in the Spanish American War Act of 1898. Spanish American War Act, ch. 187, § 1, 30 Stat. 361 (1898). Thus, by the time that the United States acquired Puerto Rico, precedents had been set for the induction of noncitizens into the American armed forces.

Noncitizens were once again made subject to the draft in 1917. The selective service statute of that year authorized the President to raise an army of several hundred thousand men. If necessary, the President was authorized to draft the required men, "[s]uch draft . . . [to] be based upon liability to military service of all male citizens, or male persons not alien enemies who have declared their intention to become citizens." Act of May 18, 1917, ch. 15, § 2, 40 Stat. 76.

It is clear that these statutes would have applied to the men of Puerto Rico even if they had not become American citizens but had remained "citizens of Porto Rico." Puerto Ricans could not have claimed the nondeclarant *alien* exemption granted by the statute because they were not aliens but nationals, *see* Gonzales v. Williams, 192 U.S. 1, 12-13 (1904); note 12 *supra*, and because that exemption was meant to accommodate the general principle of international law that aliens are not subject to military induction in the countries in which they reside. Aliens could always seek the protection of their sovereigns; Puerto Ricans, as "citizens of Porto Rico," were "entitled to the protection of the United States." Foraker Act (Puerto Rico), ch. 191, § 7, 31 Stat. 77, 79 (1900). Spain had relinquished her claim to sovereignty over Puerto Rico by the Treaty of Paris, which left "[t]he civil rights and political status of the native inhabitant . . . to . . . be determined by the Congress." Treaty of Paris, *supra* note 1, arts. II, IX. Undoubtedly, the United States, as the sovereign authority in Puerto Rico, had the power to subject these "native inhabitants" to the military draft. *See* note 46 *infra*. But cf. A. BICKEL, *supra* note 12, at 48-49 (suggesting that anyone residing within the United States may be drafted regardless of citizenship); Fitzhugh & Hyde, *The Drafting of Neutral Aliens by the United States,* 36 AM. J. INT. L. 369 (1942) (arguing that international law does not prohibit the induction of declarant aliens into military service).

[44] See note 12 *supra*.

States and were entitled to its protection. As a matter of fact, the men among the 288 persons who chose not to become citizens of the United States in accordance with the March 2, 1917 statute [45] collectively naturalizing the natives of Puerto Rico were not exempted from military duty under the Selective Service Act.[46] Finally, nothing in the annals of Congress would suggest that the collective naturalization of the Puerto Ricans was a matter connected in any way with military concerns.

The idea of American citizenship for Puerto Ricans did not arise suddenly in the Congress that enacted the Jones Act of 1917. Legislation embodying the idea had been under active and serious consideration in Congress since 1900. Inclusion of the citizenship proposal in a bill to reorganize the territorial government of Puerto Rico—a long overdue liberalization of the colonial regime supported by both major national political parties in the United States—largely explains its timing and success. One other factor doubtlessly played a role in the timing of the legislation: the adoption in late 1916, after prolonged debate, of a bill to organize the territorial government of the Philippines, which for the first time promised eventual independence to the Filipinos.[47] Only after Congress had settled the destiny of the largest of the American colonial territories was it ready to turn to the question of Puerto Rico's political fate and decide that matter free of the fear that its actions in Puerto Rico would limit its options in the Philippines.

These notes on the history of the extension of United States citizenship to Puerto Ricans are deliberately limited to a description of the congressional setting in which this legislation was con-

---

[45] *See* text accompanying notes 472 & 473 *infra.*

[46] On October 18, 1918, Major General Frank McIntyre, Chief of the Bureau of Insular Affairs in the Department of War, sent a cable to Governor Arthur Yager of Puerto Rico, informing him of the Provost Marshal General's ruling that "citizens of Puerto Rico who have declared their intention of not becoming citizens of the United States in accordance with the . . . [Jones] Act . . . , are not exempted from military duty under the Selective Service Act . . . ." Cable from Major General Frank McIntyre to Governor Arthur Yager (Oct. 18, 1918), *reprinted in* BUREAU OF SUPPLIES, PRINTING AND TRANSPORTATION, REPORT OF THE ADJUTANT GENERAL TO THE GOVERNOR OF PUERTO RICO ON THE OPERATION OF THE MILITARY REGISTRATION AND SELECTIVE DRAFT IN PUERTO RICO 93 (1924). The Adjutant General of Puerto Rico concluded "that the people of Puerto Rico, as a whole, responded most nobly and loyaly [*sic*] to the support of the United States [during World War I]." *Id.* 109. In a letter to the Adjutant General of Puerto Rico, the Provost Marshal General stated that "the percentage of delinquents and deserters on the Island is probably lower than in any other administrative sub-division." *Id.* 125.

[47] Jones Act (Philippine Islands), ch. 416, 39 Stat. 545 (1916). This statute, which bears the name of its principal congressional manager, Representative William A. Jones of Virginia, is generally known as the Jones Act of 1916 to distinguish it from the Puerto Rico statute of the following year. *See* notes 10 & 11 *supra.*

sidered for nearly two decades. No effort is here made to treat the subject in terms of public pronouncements on the subject in Puerto Rico. Although such local public statements are relevant to a comprehensive history of the island's political history, they do not, standing alone, contribute to an understanding of what happened in the one forum that truly mattered in the colonial setting—the Congress of the United States. An understanding of the congressional history of the subject may affect not only perceptions of congressional purpose and intent, but also perceptions of the historic role of the island's contemporary leadership. Perhaps most importantly, an understanding of the situation in the United States Congress in the early part of this century will provide insight into the origins of some of the contemporary political status problems of Puerto Rico.

The legislative history below will begin with an examination of the events leading to the enactment of the Foraker Act, the first organic law for Puerto Rico. Part III will discuss the Supreme Court decisions upholding the Foraker Act and trace the subsequent development of legislative proposals that culminated in the Jones Act of 1917, which, among other things, extended American citizenship to the people of Puerto Rico. The final section presents brief concluding remarks.

II. CITIZENSHIP, POLITICAL STATUS, AND THE SPECTER OF THE PHILIPPINES: PUERTO RICO AND THE GREAT DEBATE ON IMPERIALISM (1900)

The status of the inhabitants of Puerto Rico—and, of course, the political status of the island itself—was a matter of concern in Congress from the time the island became an object of American interest during the hostilities with Spain in the late 1890's. The controversy over American aims in interceding in the conflict in Cuba [48] led Congress to adopt the Teller Resolution, disclaiming "any disposition or intention to exercise sovereignty" [49] over Cuba and asserting the determination of the United States eventually to "leave the government and control of the Island to its people." [50] The sponsor of the resolution, Senator Henry M. Teller

---

[48] See H. MORGAN, AMERICA'S ROAD TO EMPIRE 62-63 (1965).

[49] H.R.J. Res. 24, 55th Cong., 2d Sess., § 4, 30 Stat. 738 (1898).

[50] Id. James Rhodes writes of the Teller Resolution:

It was offered by Senator Teller of Colorado and agreed to in the Senate without a division. It is wonderful that the United States, large and powerful, about to make war on Spain, weak and decadent, should renounce solemnly any desire to get Cuba. The fertile island, the Pearl of the Antilles, Cuba had long been coveted by America, and now when the plum was ready to drop into her mouth she abjured the wish of conquest.

of Colorado, indicated that this pledge was designed to avoid any suggestion by European powers that "when we go out to make battle for the liberty and freedom of Cuban patriots . . . we are doing it for the purpose of aggrandizement for ourselves or the increasing of our territorial holdings." [51]   This self-denying resolution, which embodied a political compromise found satisfactory by Theodore Roosevelt and other proponents of a "large policy," [52] quite clearly did not apply to other Spanish possessions, including Puerto Rico.[53]

During the invasion and trouble-free occupation of Puerto Rico on July 25, 1898, General Nelson A. Miles, commanding officer of the United States forces, issued a proclamation to the people of Puerto Rico that suggested that the island would have a direct and lasting link to the American political system.   This proclamation asserted that American forces, "bearing the banner of freedom," [54] brought to the Puerto Ricans "the fostering arm of a nation of free people, whose greatest power is in justice and humanity to all those living within its fold" [55] and promised to "bestow upon [them] the immunities and blessings of the liberal institutions of our Government . . . [and] the advantages and blessings of enlightened civilization." [56]

The implication of General Miles' proclamation, that Puerto Rico would become part of a new United States empire, was confirmed by the terms of the treaty of peace signed in Paris in 1898.[57] Under the provisions of the treaty, Spain merely abandoned "all claim of sovereignty over and title to Cuba," [58] but ceded Puerto Rico, Guam, and the Philippine Islands to the United States.[59] With respect to the question of citizenship, the treaty distinguished

---

J. Rhodes, The McKinley and Roosevelt Administrations 1897-1909, at 66-67 (1965 ed.).

[51] 31 Cong. Rec. 3897, 3899 (1898) (remarks of Sen. Teller).

[52] *See* Expansionists, *supra* note 2, at 231.

[53] Julius W. Pratt notes that "the Teller Amendment referred to Cuba alone; it said nothing of Spain's other possessions, and it is apparent that no serious expansionist felt bound to apply the spirit of the amendment elsewhere than in Cuba." *Id.* 230. C. Vann Woodward has written of the Teller resolution: "The Teller resolution proclaimed American righteousness and abstention with respect to Cuba, but as the author of the resolution carefully pointed out, it left the country a free hand 'as to some other islands,' which also belonged to Spain." C. Woodward, *supra* note 2, at 504.

[54] Constitutional History of Puerto Rico, *supra* note 8, at 55.

[55] *Id.*

[56] *Id.*

[57] Treaty of Paris, *supra* note 1.

[58] *Id.* art. I.

[59] *Id.* arts. II-III.

between "Spanish subjects, natives of the Peninsula" resident in the ceded territories, who were permitted to remain Spanish subjects upon the making of an appropriate declaration within a year's time, and "native inhabitants of the territories" who were not given this option.[60]   In the "overseas province" of Puerto Rico, the people of which had all been Spanish citizens, a clear legal distinction was thus drawn between those born in the metropolitan state and the much larger group of *criollos* or creoles who were "native inhabitants of the territories."   In addition, the treaty provided that their "civil rights and political status . . . [would] be determined by the Congress." [61]   For the first time in American history, "in a treaty acquiring territory for the United States, there was no promise of citizenship . . . [nor any] promise, actual or implied, of statehood. The United States thereby acquired not 'territories' but possessions or 'dependencies' and became, in that sense, an 'imperial' power." [62] Prior to the Treaty of Paris of 1898, "[e]very treaty by which territory was ceded to the United States . . . [had] contained some provision whereby either all or some of the inhabitants of the ceded territory could, either immediately or ultimately, be admitted to United States citizenship." [63]   In each of these earlier instances of territorial expansion, the grant or promise of citizenship to the people of a territory had clearly been regarded as a mark of the permanence of the annexation and as an effective promise of eventual incorpora-

---

[60] *Id.* art. IX.

[61] *Id.*

[62] Colonial Experiment, *supra* note 2, at 68 (footnote omitted).

[63] L. Gettys, *supra* note 12, at 144-45.   This pattern was established in 1803 in the treaty by which the United States purchased the Territory of Louisiana from France.   Treaty Between the United States of America and the French Republic, April 30, 1803, 8 Stat. 200, T.S. No. 86.   That treaty provided that "[t]he inhabitants of the ceded territory shall be incorporated in the Union of the United States, and admitted as soon as possible, according to the principles of the Federal constitution, to the enjoyment of all the rights, advantages and immunities of citizens of the United States." *Id.* art. III, 8 Stat. at 202.   Similar provisions were included in the treaties by which the United States acquired Florida, Treaty of Amity, Settlement and L'mits Between the United States and His Catholic Majesty, February 22, 1819, United States-Spain, art. 6, 8 Stat. 252, T.S. No. 327; California, Treaty of Guadalupe Hidalgo, February 2, 1848, United States-Mexico, art. VIII, 9 Stat. 922, T.S. No. 207; Arizona, Gadsden Treaty, December 30, 1853, United States-Mexico, art. V, 10 Stat. 1031, T.S. No. 208; and Alaska, Convention Ceding Alaska, March 30, 1867, United States-Russia, art. III, 15 Stat. 539, T.S. No. 301. In the case of Hawaii, which was formally annexed effective August 12, 1898, J. Res. 55, 55th Cong., 2d Sess., 30 Stat. 750 (1898), Congress in 1900 provided "[t]hat all persons who were citizens of the Republic of Hawaii on August twelfth, eighteen hundred and ninety-eight, are hereby declared to be citizens of the United States and citizens of the Territory of Hawaii."   Act of April 30, 1900, ch. 339, § 4, 31 Stat. 141.   Collective naturalization of the inhabitants of a territory or sovereign state may also be accomplished by its admission to statehood. L. Gettys, *supra* note 12, at 143.

tion of the territory as a state of the American Union. In the aftermath of the Spanish-American War, neither Congress nor the courts were persuaded by the argument that the inhabitants of these newly acquired possessions had either automatically become United States citizens upon annexation or that Congress was constitutionally compelled to confer citizenship upon them as a condition of the exercise of sovereignty. The United States had become a colonial power.

A. *America's First Experiment with Colonial Administration*

The original plans of the McKinley administration and the Republican congressional leadership for Puerto Rico seemed to call for the island's "incorporation" into the United States—that is, annexation of Puerto Rico as an integral part of the United States and the bestowal of a constitutional and political status comparable to other American territories destined for statehood.[64] Incorporation was implicit in the proposals of President McKinley's commission to study conditions in Puerto Rico; this report, completed in 1899, recommended free trade between Puerto Rico and the United States and the grant of United States citizenship to the island's inhabitants.[65] The military government in Puerto Rico, which presumably reflected the position of the national administration, called for the adoption of the free trade principle, and, in a message to Congress in December 1899, President McKinley asked for free trade legislation.[66] Although the President did not explicitly advert to the question of United States citizenship for Puerto Ricans in his message, this omission does not necessarily suggest that citizenship was not part of the administration's program. At the time it was widely believed that the inhabitants of the territories ceded by Spain had automatically become citizens of the United States,[67] as

---

[64] The possibility that a territory might be acquired but not "incorporated" into the United States was raised by Abbott Lawrence Lowell in an influential article published in the *Harvard Law Review*. Lowell, *The Status of Our New Possessions—A Third View*, 13 HARV. L. REV. 155 (1899).

[65] SPECIAL COMMISSION FOR THE UNITED STATES TO PORTO RICO, THE ISLAND OF PORTO RICO 59-61, 63 (1899).

[66] President McKinley originally stated that it was Congress' "plain duty to abolish all customs tariffs between the United States and Porto Rico." 33 CONG. REC. 36 (1899) (address of Pres. McKinley).

[67] *See, e.g.,* 33 CONG. REC. 2046 (1900) (remarks of Rep. Henry); *id.* 2064 (1900) (remarks of Rep. McClellan); *id.* 2158 (1900) (remarks of Rep. Sulzer). *See* Baldwin, *The Constitutional Questions Incident to the Acquisition and Government by the United States of Island Territory*, 12 HARV. L. REV. 393, 406-07 (1899) (espousing the view that all Puerto Rican children born after the date of acquisition were American citizens). *See also* Pfeil, *The Status of Porto Ricans in Our Polity*, 30 FORUM 717 (1901); Randolph, *Constitutional Aspects of Annexation*, 12 HARV. L. REV. 291, 300-01 (1898).

a result of the cession of the island or, in any case, that legislative action to organize a territorial government would automatically make the people of the islands American citizens. This assumption may account for President McKinley's failure to address the question directly.

Regardless of its ultimate definition or quality, citizenship was not generally objectionable to proponents of a "large policy," although it was vehemently opposed by some anti-imperialists. In any event, some congressional leaders assumed that the question of the civil status of the inhabitants of the insular possessions would ultimately be resolved not by legislative action but by a ruling of the United States Supreme Court.[68]

Citizenship was far from anathema to the McKinley administration's spokesmen in Congress who promoted and pursued the expansionist policy leading to the acquisition of the Philippines and Puerto Rico. This much is well illustrated by the original views expressed by congressional leaders on colonial questions. Representative Sereno E. Payne and Senator Joseph B. Foraker, who undoubtedly expressed the prevailing Republican opinion on the disposition of the new territories,[69] both originally favored free trade between Puerto Rico and the United States—a position that implied the annexation or incorporation of the island as an integral part of the United States. Indeed, Senator Foraker almost immediately proposed legislation explicitly providing for the grant of American citizenship to Puerto Ricans.[70]

Within a short period of time, however, both Payne and Foraker reversed their positions on free trade, and Foraker rather suddenly abandoned his citizenship proposal. These moves were gen-

---

[68] *See, e.g.,* Address by Senator Foraker, The Union League of Philadelphia (Apr. 21, 1900), *reprinted in* 33 CONG. REC. 4853 (1900).

[69] Senator Foraker and Representative Payne were the majority leaders of the Senate and House, respectively.

[70] In response to President McKinley's annual message to Congress in December 1899, Senator Joseph B. Foraker of Ohio, Republican chairman of the Senate Committee on Pacific Islands and Porto Rico, introduced S. 2264, a bill providing for American citizenship for the Puerto Ricans and for the establishment of a civil government. S. 2264, 56th Cong., 1st Sess., 33 CONG. REC. 702 (1900). (Puerto Rico was under military government from 1898 until May 1, 1900. T. CLARK, PUERTO RICO AND THE UNITED STATES, 1917-1933, at 3-4 (1975).) For the early views of Senator Foraker and his colleagues on these questions, see S. REP. No. 249, 56th Cong., 1st Sess. 13 (1900).

In the House, Representative Sereno E. Payne, Republican chairman of the House Ways and Means Committee, submitted H.R. 6883, a bill providing for free trade between the United States and Puerto Rico. H.R. 6883, 56th Cong., 1st Sess., 33 CONG. REC. 1010 (1900).

erally assumed to reflect a change in the administration's policy.[71] The reversal prompted repeated requests on the floor of the House and the Senate for a clarification of President McKinley's position. Even some expansionist Republicans were outraged by what they considered a surrender to the anti-imperialist opposition. It was reported to the Senate, for example, that the Republican Governor of Rhode Island, Elisha Dyer, had termed the raising of a tariff barrier on trade with Puerto Rico one of the most "outrageous transactions" [72] and a breach of loyalty to the principles enunciated by the Republican Party.[73] The opposition repeatedly chided the Republican leadership in Congress about the difference between their original proposals, and those of the President, and the revisions treating Puerto Rico as something other than an integral part of the United States and denying citizenship to its inhabitants.[74]

The principal reason [75] for this dramatic policy change was apparently the concern that legislation for Puerto Rico would be

---

[71] Senator George L. Wellington of Maryland termed the changes in the proposed legislation "a political somersault the like of which had not been witnessed in a generation." 33 CONG. REC. 3687 (1900) (remarks of Sen. Wellington). He added that despite the President's recommendation for free trade between the United States and Puerto Rico, "in a mysterious manner it began to be whispered that [a 15% duty on this trade] . . . was satisfactory to the Administration." *Id.*

[72] Speech by Governor Elisha Dyer delivered at Providence, Rhode Island (Mar. 31, 1900), *reprinted in* 33 CONG. REC. 3687 (1900).

[73] *Id.* Republican Representative Littlefield of Maine accused his party of "violating its faith with Puerto Rico" by virtue of its reversal on the issue of free trade. 33 CONG. REC. app. 62 (remarks of Rep. Littlefield).

[74] *See, e.g.,* 33 CONG. REC. 2158-60 (1900) (remarks of Rep. Sulzer); *id.* 2161-62 (remarks of Rep. Williams); *id.* 2264-65 (colloquy between Reps. Burke and Boutell).

[75] In the congressional debates, Republican sponsors of the tariff measure tended to justify the bill as one intended solely to benefit Puerto Rico. Representative Payne asserted that internal revenue taxes, the alternative means of raising needed funds, "would simply have destroyed [local] industries and would not have given us any appreciable revenue, no money for schools, no money for highways, no money for anything except the hard, stern realities of governing those people." *Id.* 1942 (remarks of Rep. Payne). The need for revenue was considered all the more pressing because of extensive damage caused by a recent hurricane.

> Puerto Rico is in a deplorable condition . . . [with] two-thirds of the current wealth of the island . . . destroyed by the recent hurricane. The people need immediate relief. Revenues must be obtained from some source to pay the expenses of government and provide schools for a people nine-tenths of whom can not read or write.

Id. 2051 (remarks of Rep. Long).

Democratic opponents of the Foraker Bill were less charitable in assessing the reasons for the Republican turnabout. Although many believed the Philippine difficulty to be the motive for the change, some saw no more than the majority party's reluctance to raise necessary revenues out of the treasury during an election year. *Id.* 2161 (remarks of Rep. Williams). Others, however, repeatedly accused the Republicans of succumbing to far more sinister pressures. According to Representative Sulzer:

a precedent for the larger and more menacing problem of the Philippines. It was also feared that the Puerto Rico legislation would be the subject of portentous constitutional litigation challenging congressional power to regulate trade with and migration from the insular territories, as well as the capacity of the legislative branch to determine whether Puerto Ricans and Filipinos would become United States citizens.

Concern about the possible effects of making the Philippines an integral part of the United States was not at all new in 1900. This concern had been the basis of much of the vocal opposition to McKinley's policy toward Spain and to the original decision to require the cession of the Philippines to the United States as part of the peace settlement.[76] Indeed, only a week after approving the Treaty of Paris by the slimmest possible margin [77]—one vote above the necessary two-thirds majority—the Senate had adopted a resolution declaring that it was "not intended to incorporate the inhabitants of the Philippine Islands into citizenship of the United States" [78] nor "to permanently annex said islands as an integral part of the territory of the United States," [79] but rather, to prepare the Philippines for "local self-government, and in due time to make such disposition of said islands as will best promote the interests of the citizens of the United States and the inhabitants of said islands." [80] Although the House failed to act upon this Senate initiative, it is an important and revealing expression of congressional sentiment at the zenith of the expansionist movement.

In enacting legislation for Puerto Rico, Congress sought to establish its plenary power to legislate for the government of the new territories, and to ensure its ability to deny American citizenship to the Filipinos and to regulate the entry of Filipinos and their products into the United States. Thus, the members of Congress were eager to legislate for Puerto Rico in a manner that would leave

---

Why, then, was the change made? Well, it is said, and not denied, that the majority of the Ways and Means Committee made this change at the request of the sugar trust, the tobacco trust, and the whisky trust. I believe this to be the truth about the matter.

The agents of the trusts dictated this unjust discrimination against the citizens of Puerto Rico. . . . You dare not disobey the trusts. They own and control the Republican Party.

Id. at 2159 (remarks of Rep. Sulzer).

[76] COLONIAL EXPERIMENT, *supra* note 2, at 68-74.

[77] For a description of the Senate debate on the Treaty of Paris, see EXPANIONISTS, *supra* note 2, at 358.

[78] S.J. RES. No. 240, 55th Cong., 3d Sess., 32 CONG. REC. 1846 (1899).

[79] *Id.*

[80] *Id.*

no doubt about Congress' powers under the Constitution to do with the newly acquired territories as it wished. Congressional authority to govern and administer the nation's territories during the century of expansion across a great continent had rested on constitutional guidance no more clear or instructive than the terms of the "territorial clause" of the Constitution: "The Congress shall have Power to dispose of and make all needful Rules and Regulations respecting the Territory or other Property belonging to the United States . . . ." [81] But in exercising its broad and virtually unlimited power over territories, Congress before 1898 had invariably legislated for people who were clearly a part of a definable American political community—people who were American citizens or who had been promised citizenship, and who had every expectation that their territory would, in time, be admitted as one of the states of the Union.[82] Clearly, the Puerto Rican situation was altogether novel; in fact, many respected leaders had serious doubts about the United States' course of action.[83] The legislation for the establishment of a civil government in Puerto Rico was the first opportunity to legislate for one of the newly acquired insular territories; it was simply an opportunity not to be missed.

---

[81] U.S. CONST. art. IV, § 3, cl. 2. Additionally, two other sources of congressional power to govern territories have been recognized by the Supreme Court: "The implied power to govern derived from the right to acquire territory; and . . . [t]he power implied from the fact the States admittedly not having the power, and the power having to exist somewhere, it must rest in the Federal Government." 1 W. WILLOUGHBY, THE CONSTITUTIONAL LAW OF THE UNITED STATES 431 (2d ed. 1929). Until the middle of the nineteenth century, however, "the chief reliance for the power to govern the territories had been the grant of authority contained in Article IV, Section III." *Id.* 433. The absolute congressional authority "to determine the form of political and administrative control to be erected over the Territories, and to fix the extent to which their inhabitants shall be admitted to a participation in their own government" did not necessarily "carry with it the absolute control of the Federal legislature over the civil rights—the private rights of person and property—of the inhabitants of the Territories." *Id.* 439; *cf.* Balzac v. Porto Rico, 258 U.S. 298 (1922) (United States citizens in Puerto Rico could not assert the right to trial by jury under the sixth amendment).

[82] *See* text accompanying notes 62 & 63 *supra.*

[83] American anti-expansionism antedated the Spanish-American War of 1898. Carl Schurz, a leading anti-expansionist and a charter member of the group that organized the "Anti-Imperialist Leagues" of 1898, had been arguing against American expansion into the "tropics" since the days of the Grant administration. D. HEALY, U.S. EXPANSIONISM 213-31 (1970). The anti-imperialists included E.L. Godkin, the editor of *The Nation;* Samuel Bowles, editor of the Springfield, Massachusetts *Republican;* businessmen Edward Atkinson and Charles Francis Adams, Jr.; attorney Moorfield Storey; Harvard's Charles Eliot Norton; and Andrew Carnegie. *Id.* 218-20. Included, too, were socialists, farmers, conservatives, and representatives of labor and ethnic groups. *Id.* 213-31. *See also* R. BEISNER, TWELVE AGAINST EMPIRE (1968); Harrington, *The Anti-Imperialist Movement in the United States, 1898-1900,* 22 MISS. VALLEY HIST. REV. 211 (1935).

B. *House Action on Puerto Rico: The Payne Bills (1900)*

The legislative process that culminated in the first organic statute for Puerto Rico, popularly known as the Foraker Act,[84] began in the House of Representatives on January 19, 1900, with the introduction of H.R. 6883, a bill "to extend the laws relating to customs and internal revenue over the island of Puerto Rico ceded to the United States." [85]   H.R. 6883 was introduced by Representative Payne of New York and referred to the Committee on Ways and Means, which Payne chaired.   This bill provided for free trade between Puerto Rico and the United States by treating the island, for revenue purposes, as a part of the United States.   In the month between its introduction and the commencement, on February 19, 1900,[86] of the floor debate on trade legislation for Puerto Rico, the Committee on Ways and Means substituted a new bill, H.R. 8245, "to regulate the trade of Puerto Rico, and for other purposes." [87] This second bill, also introduced and managed by Representative Payne, was radically different from his original proposal.   The second bill, like the first, contemplated the application of the tariff laws of the United States to all goods imported into Puerto Rico "from ports other than those of the United States," [88] but it also provided for the establishment of a tariff on goods imported into the United States from Puerto Rico and vice versa.[89]   In addition, the legislation that emerged from the Committee on Ways and Means provided for the segregation of customs duties on goods im-

---

[84] Foraker Act (Puerto Rico), ch. 191, 31 Stat. 77 (1900).   Joseph Benson Foraker, a Civil War veteran and lawyer, came to the Senate in 1897 from Ohio, where he served as governor and fought against the state political machine run by Mark Hanna.   After succeeding Hanna in 1906 as head of Ohio's political machine, he became something of a political power.   He openly challenged the leadership of Theodore Roosevelt during the latter's second term as president and opposed William Howard Taft's nomination in 1908.   His role as a political boss, however, was short lived.   During the presidential campaign of 1908, William Randolph Hearst published certain letters written by John D. Archbold, vice president of the Standard Oil Company, revealing that Senator Foraker had been in the company's employ while in office and had received large sums of money from Archbold.   Despite his insistence that the money represented payment for legal services to the company, Foraker was not nominated for re-election by the Ohio legislature in 1909.   Foraker died in 1917.   *Joseph B. Foraker, Ex-Senator, Dead,* N.Y. Times, May 11, 1917, § 1, at 11, col. 1; *Burton for Senator; Taft, Foraker Out,* N.Y. Times, Jan. 1, 1909, § 1, at 7, col. 1; *Taft Carries Ohio by Big Plurality,* N.Y. Times, Nov. 4, 1908, § 1, at 2, col. 3; *Foraker Out of Taft's Meeting,* N.Y. Times, Sept. 20, 1908, § 1, at 1, col. 7; *Taft-Foraker Plan May Be Abandoned,* N.Y. Times, Sept. 19, 1908, § 1, at 1, col. 1.

[85] H.R. 6883, 56th Cong., 1st Sess., 33 CONG. REC. 1010 (1900).

[86] 33 CONG. REC. 1940 (1900).

[87] H.R. REP. No. 249, 56th Cong., 1st Sess. 1, 16 (1900).

[88] H.R. 8245, § 2, 56th Cong., 1st Sess., 33 CONG. REC. 1940 (1900).

[89] *Id.* § 3.

ported from Puerto Rico into a separate fund "for the government and benefit of Puerto Rico." [90] Even before it was transformed in the Senate into legislation dealing more broadly with civil government in Puerto Rico, the substitute Payne bill triggered consideration of the basic and unresolved questions of citizenship and political status, and the all-important question whether American dominion over these territories would be temporary or permanent.

In the favorable report on the substitute Payne bill issued on February 8, 1900, the Committee on Ways and Means made only a passing reference to the question of the Philippines.[91] After an extensive review of precedents concerning the definition of "United States" and the meaning of the provisions of the Constitution granting Congress the power "to dispose of and make all needful Rules and Regulations respecting the Territory or other Property belonging to the United States," [92] the Committee offered some important conclusions as the basis for its favorable report on the substitute bill:

> First.   That upon reason and authority the term "United States," as used in the Constitution, has reference only to the States that constitute the Federal Union and does not include Territories.
>
> Second.   That the power of Congress with respect to legislation for the Territories is plenary.
>
> Third.   That under that power Congress may prescribe different rates of duty for Puerto Rico from those prescribed for the United States.[93]

The Committee's minority report expressed a different view— one that was to be echoed throughout the United States in the months to come. The substitute Payne bill, according to this perspective, was

> wholly inconsistent with the theory and form of our Government. The exercise of such power is pure and simple imperialism, and against it we enter our most solemn protest. . . . The blessings of free government rest alike upon all of our people, whether in the thirteen original States or

---

90 *Id.* § 4.

91 The committee report mentioned the Philippines only in a brief reference to the power of Congress to provide for "a discrimination which we make against no other portion of the territory belonging to the United States where the inhabitants are not in a state of insurrection." H.R. Rep. No. 249, *supra* note 87, at 6.

92 U.S. Const. art. IV, § 3, cl. 2.

93 H.R. Rep. No. 249, *supra* note 87, at 16.

in the youngest member of the Union, or in the newest acquired territory. It does not matter in which form territory is acquired, it is to be held under our Constitution with the object of finally being admitted into the Union as a State.[94]

The minority report stated for the first time the bewilderment of some members of Congress concerning the apparent change in the administration's position.[95]   The dispute within the Committee on Ways and Means on this issue was renewed on the floor of the House of Representatives on February 19, 1900, when the House considered the substitute bill.

No sooner had Representative Payne, in his opening remarks on the trade bill on the floor of the House, adverted to the good works to be done in Puerto Rico with the monies raised by the projected tariff than the momentous question of citizenship was put to him by Representative Pierce of Tennessee: "Does the gentleman believe that as soon as the ratification of the treaty of peace was made that the Puerto Ricans were citizens of the United States or does he think that they fell outside of the Constitution?"[96]   This troublesome question would appear and reappear throughout the debate on the first major legislation for Puerto Rico and would not finally be answered until the *Insular Cases*[97] were decided more than a year later.[98]   It was a question that Representative Payne wanted to avoid; he succeeded in doing so temporarily by invoking the narrow purposes of his bill: "[T]he gentleman from Tennessee ought to know that that is a question that has nothing to do with sugar."[99]   Clearly the majority leader of the House shared the view of various colleagues who wanted, from the outset, to treat Puerto Rico somewhat differently from the Philippines by offering the prospect of political integration with the United States without establishing a precedent for dealing with the Philippines. American citizenship for Puerto Ricans was a possibility, in Representative Payne's view, but he was prepared to acquiesce in the administration's decision that citizenship was not appropriate in 1900.   In

---

94 *Id.* 18.

95 *Id.* 19-20.

96 33 CONG. REC. 1943 (1900) (remarks of Rep. Pierce).

97 De Lima v. Bidwell, 182 U.S. 1 (1901); Dooley v. United States, 182 U.S. 222 (1901); Armstrong v. United States, 182 U.S. 243 (1901); Downes v. Bidwell, 182 U.S. 244 (1901).   See text accompanying notes 182-219 *infra*.

98 *See* L. Gould, The Foraker Act 47-56, 202-32 (1958) (unpublished thesis in University of Michigan Library).

99 33 CONG. REC. 1943 (1900) (remarks of Rep. Payne).

Payne's words: "Keep them all in leading strings until you have educated them up to the full stature of American manhood, and then crown them with the glory of American citizenship." [100]

A disposition to confer American citizenship on the inhabitants of Puerto Rico and to treat the cession of the island as a permanent annexation was evident among both proponents and opponents of the Payne bill; indeed, more congressmen spoke out in favor of citizenship than against it. Nevertheless, as Representative Newlands of Nevada, who had dissented in Committee, noted, the Republican majority feared

> the establishment of a precedent which [would] be invoked to control our action regarding the Philippines later on; such action embracing not simply one island near our coast, easily governed, its people friendly and peaceful [*i.e.,* Puerto Rico], but embracing an archipelago of seventeen hundred islands 7,000 miles distant, of diverse races, speaking different languages, having different customs, and ranging all the way from absolute barbarism to semicivilization.[101]

Although annexationist designs on Puerto Rico were shared by "imperialists" and "anti-imperialists" alike, the record of the congressional debates in 1900 reveals a widespread and rather special disquietude concerning the dangers of placing the inhabitants of the islands in the Orient on an equal constitutional footing with Americans. Representative Newlands, who noted that the earlier exclusion of Chinese immigrants from the United States had been based upon the realization by "thinking men . . . that American civilization was in danger," [102] felt that a similar threat was posed by the Filipinos. He perceived no such danger, however, in the case of the inhabitants of other insular possessions, including Puerto Rico:

> With reference to Puerto Rico we all agree that no great danger to the industrial system of this country can come from the acquisition of Puerto Rico. It lies there on a line to the Gulf, on the route to the future Nicaragua Canal, and comes legitimately within our scheme of expansion involving continental territory on the northern hemisphere and adjacent islands. Hawaii, Puerto Rico,

---

100 *Id.* 1946.

101 *Id.* 1994 (remarks of Rep. Newlands).

102 *Id.* 2001.

and Cuba, we all—both imperialists and anti-imperialists—agree, constitute a part of legitimate expansion of both our territory and our Government.

As to these islands in the Philippine group, 7,000 miles away, we all agree, whatever may have been the mistakes of commission or omission in the past . . . we only differ as to the ultimate disposition of those islands, as to whether they shall remain permanently a part of the United States or whether we shall hold them in trust for their own people and ultimately grant them independence. This is the only contention.

. . . .

. . . It can be easily imagined what will be the effect of putting inside of our governmental and industrial system 9,000,000 people possessing a high degree of industrial aptitude and accustomed to a scale of wages and mode of living appropriate to Asiatics.

Such are the evils of incorporating the Philippines into our governmental and industrial system . . . .[103]

Race, civilization, distance, and economic considerations formed the basis for the distinction made in Congress between Puerto Rico and the Philippines.[104] Expressions of concern about the annexation of Oriental peoples were commonplace. The statement by Representative Dalzell that he was unwilling "to see the wage-earner of the United States, the farmer of the United States, put upon a level and brought into competition with the cheap half-slave labor, savage labor, of the Philippine Archipelago"[105] was greeted by loud applause in the House. Other congressmen echoed his sentiments.[106] These statements were in marked contrast to the usual descriptions of the Puerto Ricans.[107]

---

[103] Id. Representative Newlands specifically stated that "[t]he Puerto Rico question [was] linked with the Philippine question." Id. 1994. He went on to say that "[t]he latter presents the only difficulty in the way of the solution of the relations of our newly acquired islands." Id.

[104] It is not surprising that racism was a significant factor in the debates on the disposition of the insular territories acquired from Spain. A generation earlier the Grant administration's plan to annex the Dominican Republic had failed largely because of apprehensions about the race and "civilization" of its people. See E. May, American Imperialism 99-115 (1968).

[105] 33 Cong. Rec. 1959 (1900) (remarks of Rep. Dalzell).

[106] See, e.g., id. 2072 (remarks of Rep. Brantley); id. 2105 (remarks of Rep. Spight); id. 2172 (remarks of Rep. Gilbert) (cautioning against "open[ing] wide the door by which these negroes and Asiatics can pour like the locusts of Egypt into this country").

[107] See text accompanying note 118 infra.

The relatively tender treatment accorded to the Puerto Ricans may be partially explained by the representations made in Congress concerning the racial composition of the island. For example, Representative Payne readily accepted questionable census reports showing that whites—"generally full-blooded white people, descendants of the Spaniards, possibly mixed with some Indian blood, but none of them [of] negro extraction" [108]—outnumbered by nearly two to one the combined total of Negroes and mulattoes.[109] Hawaii did not constitute a precedent for the annexation of a territory populated by people of a different race. Indeed, opponents of the annexation of the Philippines had actively supported the annexation of the Hawaiian Islands in 1898 and would support annexation of Puerto Rico. Representative Newlands, who sponsored the resolution that annexed the Hawaiian Islands,[110] made this clear during the 1900 debate on Puerto Rico:

> There were no complex problems in regard to the people occupying those islands. Only 100,000 people occupied them. They had been practically assimilated and were in sympathy with our institutions and our whole system of government. Their acquisition involved no industrial derangement in this country . . . .[111]

Whatever might be the final disposition of the matter of the Philippines, it was "evident that both of the political parties of the country [were] now in substantial agreement that Puerto Rico [would] become a part of the Union." [112] Nevertheless, it was suggested that in legislating for the government of Puerto Rico it seemed advisable to avoid any action which would impair the United States' flexibility in its future policy toward the Philippines, and in particular, action from which it might be inferred that Congress accepted the proposition that all the insular territories acquired from Spain were automatically "a part of" the United States and their peoples citizens of the United States fully entitled to all the guarantees of the Constitution.

The Puerto Ricans' lack of resistance in the face of invasion and occupation and the relative proximity of the island to the United

---

108 33 CONG. REC. 1941 (1900) (remarks of Rep. Payne).

109 *Id.*

110 Act of July 7, 1898, H.R.J. Res. No. 259, 30 Stat. 750. The measure was originally introduced by Rep. Newlands on May 4, 1898. 31 CONG. REC. 4600 (1898).

111 33 CONG. REC. 2000-01 (1900) (remarks of Rep. Newlands).

112 *Id.* 1994 (remarks of Rep. Newlands).

States formed additional grounds for distinguishing beween the Philippines and Puerto Rico. Representative Jacob H. Bromwell, an Ohio Republican, who had little doubt that the Puerto Ricans were "as a whole, of a higher grade of civilization than the Filipinos," [113] noted that "[t]he circumstances surrounding the Philippines and Puerto Rico are very different" [114] and compelled different treatment.

> Puerto Rico came to us voluntarily and without bloodshed. She welcomed us with open arms. Her adherence to the United States during the Spanish war saved the loss, possibly, of many lives and the expenditure of millions of money. Her people welcomed the armies under Miles as deliverers and benefactors. They professed themselves ready to become peaceable and loyal citizens of this country. . . . They are orderly, law abiding, and anxious for development. . . . If any people on earth deserve fair and considerate treatment at our hands it is the people of Puerto Rico.
>
> . . . .
>
> But it is said that this is the first of our new colonial possessions for which we are called upon to legislate, and in order to show our assertion of authority we must make an example of Puerto Rico; and that we are anxious to have a test case made before the Supreme Court to find out just what authority we have in legislating on our new possessions, and that we can use Puerto Rico for the purpose.
>
> It is as if, doubtful how far I might go in disciplining one refractory son, I thrash an obedient one in the hope that if arrested a police magistrate may define to me just how far I may safely go in my parental castigation in the future. [Applause.]
>
> . . . .
>
> We propose, in this way, to establish a precedent for the Filipinos, the unruly and disobedient, by disciplining and punishing Puerto Rico, the well-behaved and well-disposed.[115]

Another opponent of the substitute Payne bill, Representative George B. McClellan of New York, an avowed anti-imperialist,

---

[113] *Id.* 2043 (remarks of Rep. Bromwell).
[114] *Id.*
[115] *Id.*

argued for free trade between Puerto Rico and the United States. McClellan favored making a distinction between the Philippines and Puerto Rico—a distinction under which Puerto Rico would be regarded as a part of the United States, and not merely its possession, and its people would be citizens of the United States.

> Puerto Rico belongs to us, and it is a problem that must be solved now. It is a part of the United States; the Constitution extends over it; its territory is our territory; its people are our citizens. . . . The case of Puerto Rico is very different from that of the Philippines, for its inhabitants are few and capable of education; they are peaceful and are anxious to obtain the blessings of American civilization, and what is more, they are at our very doors.
>
> I believe that we can only hold territory, as a nation, in trust for the States that are ultimately to be erected out of that territory. I believe that we can only hold the territory of Puerto Rico in trust for the sovereign State that will be some day admitted into the Union. We are only dealing with Puerto Rico now, and yet the majority see in the proposition an endless skein of complications, for they know that, however they may disguise it, they propose to hold the Philippines in perpetual servitude.[116]

Representative Thomas Spight of Mississippi distinguished between the Philippines and Puerto Rico in an almost stereotypical fashion and combined the usual arguments about geographical proximity and the alleged racial similarity of Puerto Ricans to white Americans with the injunctions of the Monroe Doctrine. Puerto Rico could be a part of the United States, and its people citizens of the United States, because Puerto Rico was located within a traditional American sphere of influence—"in a measure, contiguous territory. It is a part of the American continent." [117]

> Its people are, in the main, of Caucasian blood, knowing and appreciating the benefits of civilization, and are desirous of casting their lot with us. . . .
>
> How different the case of the Philippine Islands, 10,000 miles away . . . . The inhabitants are of wholly different races of people from ours—Asiatics, Malays, negroes and mixed blood. They have nothing in common with us and centuries can not assimilate them. . . . They can never be clothed with the rights of American citizen-

---

116 *Id.* 2067 (remarks of Rep. McClellan).

117 *Id.* 2105 (remarks of Rep. Spight).

ship nor their territory admitted as a State of the American
Union . . . .

. . . .

But the case is essentially different with Puerto Rico.
Its proximity to our mainland, the character of its inhabitants, and the willingness with which they accept our sovereignty, together with the advantages—commercial, sani-
tary and strategic—all unite to enable us to make her an
integral part of our domain, without any violence to principle or any danger of foreign entanglements.[118]

Imperialists and anti-imperialists alike could (and did) appreciate differences between Puerto Rico and the Philippines. Sentiment favoring the view that Puerto Ricans were already American
citizens—and therefore, that Puerto Rico was already "a part of"
the United States, to which the Constitution was fully applicable—
was especially strong among the anti-imperialists. Among the imperialists who might be disposed toward the incorporation of Puerto
Rico, however, there remained a concern that legislation for Puerto
Rico necessarily established a precedent for the Philippines; that the
treatment of Puerto Rico as an incorporated territory ("a part of"
the United States) would mean a similar status for the Philippines;
and that free trade between Puerto Rico and the United States
might mean free trade between the Philippines and the United
States. "I understand full well," asserted Representative William E.
Williams of Illinois, "that the Administration does not care a fig for
Puerto Rico; that this precedent is about to be established not for
the mere sake of deriving a revenue from that island, but as a precedent for our future guidance in the control of the Philippines." [119]

The debate in the House on the Payne bill was concluded on
February 28, 1900, nine days after it had begun. The first order of
business was the disposition of a substitute bill offered by Representative Samuel W. McCall of Massachusetts,[120] an outspoken advocate of granting United States citizenship to the inhabitants of
Puerto Rico.[121] The McCall bill called for a revival of the original
Payne proposal whereby Congress would merely have "extended to
and over the island of Puerto Rico" the "laws of the United States
relating to customs and internal revenue." [122] It is not at all cer-

---

118 *Id.*
119 *Id.* 2162 (remarks of Rep. Williams).
120 *Id.* 2428 (House vote).
121 *Id.* 2092.
122 *Id.* 2428.

tain what effect such a bill would have had on the question of the citizenship of Puerto Ricans. This much is clear: it was the constitutional premise of the substitute Payne bill that Puerto Rico was not an integral part of the United States and that Congress therefore was not bound by the requirement of article I, section 8 of the Constitution that "all Duties, Imposts and Excises shall be uniform throughout the United States." [123] Although neither the substitute Payne bill nor the McCall bill directly referred to the citizenship of Puerto Ricans, only the McCall bill left open the question whether Puerto Rico was a part of the United States and, if so, whether its people were citizens of the United States. Merely by extending the customs and revenue laws of the United States to Puerto Rico, the McCall bill would have strengthened the view that such uniformity was constitutionally required; it would have permitted an inference that uniformity was required because Puerto Rico was an integral part of the United States and its inhabitants arguably were citizens of the United States.

On February 28, 1900, the McCall bill was defeated by a vote of 174 to 160.[124] By a nearly identical margin the House promptly defeated a motion to recommit the substitute Payne bill to the Committee on Ways and Means.[125] Following the failure of these preliminary attempts to defeat it, the substitute Payne bill was passed by a vote of 172 to 160.[126]

C. *Senate Action on Puerto Rico: The Foraker Bill (1900)*

The original bill [127] considered by the Senate Committee on Pacific Islands and Puerto Rico, and reported favorably on February 5, 1900,[128] would have treated Puerto Rico as part of the United States solely for revenue and customs purposes, by extending internal revenue and related tax laws and by providing for duty-free trade between Puerto Rico and the continental United States.[129] As the Committee reported, the bill "[did] not . . . extend the Constitution of the United States." [130] Only three days after the Senate Committee's report, the House Committee on Ways and Means re-

---

[123] U.S. CONST. art. I, § 8 cl. 1.

[124] 33 CONG. REC. 2428 (1900) (House vote).

[125] *Id.* 2429.

[126] *Id.* 2429-30 (House vote).

[127] S. 2264, 56th Cong., 1st Sess., (1900) (unamended version) (text on file in Library of Congress); *see* 33 CONG. REC. 1486 (1900).

[128] S. REP. No. 249, *supra* note 70.

[129] S. 2264, *supra* note 127, §§ 7, 8, 35.

[130] S. REP. No. 249, *supra* note 70, at 4.

ported favorably on H.R. 8245,[131] Payne's substitute bill, which made no suggestion that Puerto Rico was an "incorporated" territory. In view of the change in administration policy then apparently underway, it is not surprising that by the time the Senate was ready to act on the Puerto Rico bill in the first days of March, 1900, the original Foraker bill, S. 2264, like the original Payne bill, had been scrapped.[132] The Senate thus considered the bill adopted by the House, as now amended by the Chairman of the Committee on Pacific Islands and Puerto Rico, Senator Foraker of Ohio. While incorporating the substance of the revenue bill approved by the House, the Senate bill also sought to establish a civil government on the island.[133] Moreover, the Senate bill provided for the collective grant of American citizenship to those inhabitants of the island who were Spanish subjects on April 11, 1899 [134] and their afterborn progeny, if such persons continued to reside in Puerto Rico and had not elected to preserve their Spanish nationality in accordance with the terms of the Treaty of Paris.[135]

Despite the projected grant of American citizenship to the Puerto Ricans, the bill clearly did not make Puerto Rico an integral part of the United States or extend to its inhabitants the full panoply of individual rights guaranteed by the Constitution. Citizenship was offered neither as a means of having the Constitution "follow the flag," nor as a confirmation that the Constitution did follow the flag.[136] There was nothing remarkable about the bill or its citizenship provision, in the view of Senator Foraker, "except only that its provisions are of such a character as to recognize that Puerto Rico *belongs to the United States of America.*" [137] The author of the first legislative proposal to make Puerto Ricans citizens of the United States thus acknowledged, as others would in the years to come, that the principal objective of granting American citizenship to Puerto Ricans was neither to incorporate Puerto Rico into the United States (and thereby to have the Constitution apply in all respects to the island and its people) nor to grant Puerto Ricans political and civil rights equal to those of citizens in the

---

[131] H.R. 8245, *supra* note 88; *see* text accompanying notes 90-95 *supra*.

[132] *See* note 68 *supra*.

[133] S. 2264, *supra* note 127.

[134] This was the date of the exchange of ratifications of the treaty between Spain and the United States. Treaty of Paris, *supra* note 1.

[135] S. 2264, *supra* note 127; S. Rep. No. 249, *supra* note 70. *See* Treaty of Paris, *supra* note 1, art. IX.

[136] 33 Cong. Rec. 2473-74 (1900) (remarks of Sen. Foraker).

[137] *Id.* 2473 (emphasis added).

American Union proper. The objective, rather, was "to recognize that Puerto Rico *belongs to the United States of America.*" [138]

Although the question of citizenship was linked to the island's political status, it had little or nothing to do with individual rights or, in particular, with entitlement to participation in the political or electoral processes of the United States. Senator Foraker noted:

> We considered very carefully what status in a political sense we would give to the people of [Puerto Rico], and we reported that provision not thoughtlessly. . . . We concluded . . . that the inhabitants of that island must be either citizens or subjects or aliens. We did not want to treat our own as aliens, and we do not propose to have any subjects. Therefore, we adopted the term "citizens." *In adopting the term "citizens" we did not understand, however, that we were giving to those people any rights that the American people do not want them to have.* "Citizens" is a word that indicates, according to Story's work on the Constitution of the United States, allegiance on the one hand and protection on the other.[139]

After a reference to the limited privileges and immunities ascribed by Justice Story to the citizens of the states, Senator Foraker reiterated his earlier remarks in a colloquy with a colleague on the floor of the Senate. Senator Foraker underscored the difference between a grant of citizenship and the conferral of individual rights under the Constitution of the United States by noting that the term "citizen," when "used in the political sense," was an "unimportant" one that described a "person owing allegiance to the government and entitled to protection from it." [140] Accordingly, he stated that the citizenship clause in the bill "confer[red] the right to vote or to participate in the government upon no one." [141] Whether the Constitution applied to newly acquired territories was therefore a different issue from that of the grant of citizenship. Senator Foraker fully shared the views held by Representative Payne and the proponents of the House bill that the legislative branch was endowed by the Constitution and by the terms of the Treaty of Paris with "plenary power to do in this matter as Congress may

---

138 *Id.* (emphasis added).

139 *Id.* (emphasis added). *Cf.* note 12 *supra* (on the status of *nationals* as distinguished from *citizens*).

140 *Id.* 2474 (remarks of Sen. Foraker) (quoting Justice Story).

141 *Id.*

see fit." [142] This position, later confirmed by the Supreme Court,[143] for a generation would underlie congressional discussion of American citizenship for the Puerto Ricans.

The Senate debate on the Foraker bill revealed widespread agreement among opponents as well as proponents of the bill that Congress had the plenary power to legislate for "unincorporated" territories. The record, therefore, reveals substantially less apprehension among the members of the Senate than among the members of the House about the precedential significance of the Puerto Rico legislation for the Philippines. Senator Lindsay of Kentucky, for example, was "not afraid to be just to and liberal and generous with the people of this American island on the ground that we may establish a precedent to be used against us when we come to determine the civil rights and the political status of the Filipinos." [144] He also felt that making Puerto Ricans American citizens would "place us under no obligation, constitutional or otherwise, to follow that course when we come to legislate concerning the Tagals, Malays, etc., who inhabit the islands of the Philippine Archipelago." [145] Senator Teller of Colorado, a leading Senate figure on colonial questions, intimated that he favored colonial status for both Puerto Rico and the Philippines,[146] but he stated that he saw no binding precedent for the Philippines in anything Congress might do with respect to Puerto Rico.[147]

The fear that legislation for Puerto Rico would set a precedent for the disposition of the Philippines question was clearly articulated during the Senate debate on the Foraker bill, albeit with greater subtlety than in the House. One of the few explicit remarks on the subject was made by Senator Turner of Washington. He felt that in the preparation of the Foraker bill "it has been found necessary to make a vicious and tyrannical precedent toward [Puerto

---

[142] Id. 2475.

[143] See text accompanying notes 182-218 infra; Balzac v. Porto Rico, 258 U.S. 298 (1922).

[144] 33 CONG. REC. 2696 (1900) (remarks of Sen. Lindsay).

[145] Id.

[146] Id. 2471 (remarks of Sen. Teller regarding Puerto Rico); id. 6510 (remarks of Sen Teller regarding the Philippines). Although Teller saw "no reason . . . why the United States may not have a colony," he felt that the nation was bound to extend to any colony the "great principles that underlie free government and to maintain there a free government and to maintain liberty." Id. 2471.

[147] Id. 2472. But even Teller recognized that the "influence [legislation for Puerto Rico] may have upon future legislation touching the Asiatic islands may be very important." Id.

Rico] which will hereafter bar out the labor and the products of the Philippine Islands." [148]

As in the House, the Senate debate also focused on larger questions of general imperial policy. Thus the debate was frequently filled with racist rhetoric. It is ironic, but not surprising, that racist overtones were most clearly discernible in the remarks of those who opposed American imperialism [149] and argued most strenuously that "[s]ubjects do not exist in a free republic." [150] It was often left to the proponents of colonialism and annexation to extol the virtue and dignity of the colonial peoples whom they sought to bring, and keep, under the American flag. The anti-colonial views expressed by Senator Bate of Tennessee were widely shared. He asserted that the question of Puerto Rico's future, "[l]eft alone, without being associated with other interests, . . . could be disposed of very readily, and there would perhaps be but little trouble and less excitement and sensational feeling in our country in regard to it." [151] Senator Bate also asserted, however, that "[t]he truth in connection with this . . . is that there is something behind Porto Rico which is mightier than the Porto Rican question." [152]

> [T]here is evidently behind [the debate on Puerto Rico] a political dagger in [the] shape of the Philippines. That is the objective of this battle. No one who has witnessed the scenes that have taken place in this Chamber; no one who has read the current criticisms of the newspapers of the day; no one who has read the messages of the President and the communications of the Secretary of War and other officials connected herewith, but knows and feels in his heart that *there is something behind this more mighty than is this proposition touching the government of Porto Rico. The Philippines are behind it with all their troubles. That is like Pandora's box, full of ills, some of which are upon us, and others are to come. That is the real question. Porto Rico is but its front shadow.*
>
> *Yes, Porto Rico could be readily settled, easily disposed of, but for that which is to come after it. The embarrassing question is as to the character of government that we are to have in the Philippines and how it will affect certain*

---

148 *Id.* 2813 (remarks of Sen. Turner).
149 *See, e.g., id.* 3613, 3616 (1900) (remarks of Sen. Bate).
150 *Id.* 3610.
151 *Id.* 3608.
152 *Id.*

*interests. We are upon that line of battle to-day [sic],
under cover.* Able and astute politicians of this Senate,
especially those who represent and lead the other side of
this Chamber, see that it is necessary to fight this battle
upon the Porto Rican line, and not on that of the Orient.
They have so decided, and hence the battle has been made
here, although there is a bill . . . upon the table which
involves the other question in regard to the character of
the government that we are to have in the Philippines.

Then the Porto Rican question and the Philippine
question is the same thing, and this has been brought about
very shrewdly and adroitly by the leading spirits—those
who think and mold and lead the movements of the
Republican party of the country.[153]

Senator Bate, an anti-imperialist, believed that "[t]he Constitution of our country extends wherever the flag goes,"[154] and that
"[s]ubjects do not exist in a free republic."[155] Bate saw in the proposed legislation a "singular likeness" to the policy of England toward the American colonies and feared that "the omnipotence of
Congress [asserted by the Puerto Rico bill] produces the same fruit
as the absolutism of the English Parliament."[156]

The political roots of this anti-imperialism, particularly among
populist and Southern legislators, lay partly in a preoccupation with
the race of the colonial peoples and not solely in concern for
libertarian ideals and constitutional principles. Thus, Senator Bate
adverted to reports that some Filipinos were "physically weaklings
of low stature, with black skin, closely curling hair, flat noses, thick
lips, and large, clumsy feet."[157] He doubted that the precedent of
"expanding our authority once to the Europeans living in Louisiana
can be deemed as sustaining the incorporation of millions of savages,
cannibals, Malays, Mohammedans, head hunters, and polygamists
into even the subjects of an American Congress."[158]

> Let us not take the Philippines in our embrace to keep
> them simply because we are able to do so. I fear it would
> prove a serpent in our bosom. Let us beware of those
> mongrels of the East, with breath of pestilence and touch
> of leprosy. Do not let them become a part of us with

---

153 *Id.*
154 *Id.* 3609.
155 *Id.* 3610.
156 *Id.* 3614.
157 *Id.* 3613.
158 *Id.*

their idolatry, polygamous creeds, and harem habits. Charity begins at home, Mr. President, and let us beware! I fear we are eating sour grapes and our children's teeth will be on edge.[159]

Unlike Senator Bate, proponents of the Foraker bill such as Senator Depew of New York saw Puerto Rico as an island with which the United States might have an honorable and fruitful association: "With capital, enterprise, and modern machinery the possibilities of increase in its productiveness can not be calculated."[160] However, even they were fully prepared to accept the proposition that the United States could not and would not "incorporate the alien races, and civilized, semi-civilized, barbarous, and savage peoples of these islands into our body politic as States of our Union."[161] The answer they offered to the anti-imperialists like Senator Bate was neither the promise of incorporation nor the avoidance of political and moral duty; the answer was to retain the new insular territories as possessions or colonies of the United States.[162]

Despite Senator Foraker's assertion that there was no inconsistency between the grant of American citizenship and the clear understanding that Puerto Rico would not become an integral part of the United States, a single, moderately worded attack upon the citizenship provision by Senator Teller at the end of the second week of debate on the bill was most influential. Teller argued that "[i]f [the Puerto Ricans] are a part of the United States, if their people are citizens of the United States, you have no right to put a duty upon their goods. If they are not citizens of the United States, then it is a question of policy and not a question of justice."[163] On March 19, 1900 Senator Foraker responded by proposing an amendment to the Senate bill that deleted the reference to citizenship of the United States and substituted a provision that Puerto Ricans would be "citizens of Puerto Rico, and as such entitled to the protection of the United States."[164] Nearly a fortnight later, he explained the proposal to eliminate United States citizenship as one prompted by the suggestion that the grant of American citizenship would have the effect of making Puerto Rico an incorporated

---

159 *Id.* 3616.
160 *Id.* 3619 (remarks of Sen. Depew).
161 *Id.* 3622.
162 *Id.*
163 *Id.* 2875 (remarks of Sen. Teller).
164 *Id.* 3037 (remarks of Sen. Foraker).

territory rather than a dependency or possession.[165] The citizenship provision was therefore eliminated in order to avoid conveying the idea "that we were incorporating [Puerto Rico] into the Union . . . thus putting it in a state of pupilage for statehood." [166]

Senator Foraker claimed that the change in the position of the Republican administration and the Republican leadership in Congress was based simply on increased awareness of economic and social conditions in Puerto Rico and a realization of the need to raise revenue for the new civil government.[167] The revised bills envisaged the establishment of a special fund from monies collected by the proposed tariff on trade to and from Puerto Rico, all of which would be used for the support of this new government.[168] In Senator Foraker's view, the need to raise funds for the new insular government "without our practicing paternalism to the extent of feeding them from day to day out of our public Treasury" [169] compelled the abandonment of the original citizenship provision. Despite the need to raise revenue for the government of Puerto Rico,

> it did not at all necessarily follow that they should not be[come] citizens of the United States, as I originally proposed in my bill, but every Democratic Senator almost, without exception, was saying that if we made them citizens of the United States we thereby made them a part of the United States, and if we made them a part of the United States that provision of the Constitution with respect to uniform taxation would apply, and we could not raise revenue in the way proposed in this bill. It was Democratic opposition, Mr. President, that brought us to realize that there ought to be a change from our original proposition, as it was clearly within the power of Congress to make it in the civil and political status of the people of Porto Rico. That is the complete explanation of the change which has been made. It was for that reason and no other.[170]

---

165 *Id.* 3554.

166 *Id.*

167 *Id.* 3690-91.

168 *Id.* 3576.

169 *Id.* 3690.

170 *Id.* *But see* note 265 *infra* & accompanying text (Senator Foraker's later (1906) explanation of these events). *See also* note 68 *supra*.

Foraker's amendments to the citizenship provisions of his Committee's bill were adopted by voice vote on April 3, 1900.[171] That same day the Senate adopted an amendment, also proposed by Foraker, to delete a provision for the election of a non-voting Delegate to the House of Representatives of the United States,[172] a position comparable to that held by elected representatives of "incorporated" territories such as Arizona, New Mexico, and Hawaii.[173] In its place, the Senate adopted an amendment offered by Foraker that provided for the election of a "resident commissioner to the United States, who shall be entitled to official recognition as such by all Departments, upon presentation to the Department of State of a certificate of election of the governor of Porto Rico." [174] The resident commissioner would not be given a seat in the House of Representatives. Although in 1904 the position of resident commissioner became functionally equivalent to that of Delegate,[175] the form of its creation and the manner of accreditation were more akin to that of an ambassadorship from a foreign land.

On April 3, 1900, after the defeat of a motion to substitute the original bill that Foraker had brought to the Senate floor on March 2, the amended bill was passed on a rollcall vote of 40 to 31.[176] On

---

171 *Id.* 3693 (Senate vote).

172 *Id.*

173 *See generally* 2 HINDS' PRECEDENTS OF THE HOUSE OF REPRESENTATIVES, ch. XLIII, §§ 1290-96 (1907) [hereinafter cited as HINDS' PRECEDENTS].

174 33 CONG. REC. 3693 (1900) (amendment offered by Sen. Foraker). It should be noted, however, that at this time, prior to the Federal Register Act of 1935, 44 U.S.C. §§ 301-314 (1976), the State Department served as a general repository for government documents, including all federal regulations. *See* 1 K. DAVIS, ADMINISTRATIVE LAW TREATISE, § 6.09, at 393 (1958). President Thomas Jefferson first gave the State Department supervisory authority over all territories of the United States in the year 1793, and the Department retained exclusive competence in this area until 1873. Pomeroy, *The American Colonial Office*, 30 MISS. VALLEY HIST. REV. 521, 521-22 (1943).

175 *See* HINDS' PRECEDENTS, *supra* note 173, at § 1306.

176 33 CONG. REC. 3697-98 (1900) (Senate vote). In its final form the Foraker Act was far more extensive than a simple revenue measure; it was, in fact, an "Organic Act" establishing a civil government for the island of Puerto Rico, passed, not by Puerto Ricans, but by the United States Congress. The bill provided for the appointment of a governor of Puerto Rico by the President of the United States; the appointment of an eleven man executive council, five members of which were to be Puerto Rican, to serve as an upper house of the legislative branch as well as the governor's cabinet; and the establishment of a thirty-five member popularly elected House of Delegates. The island was entitled to elect a resident commissioner to Washington.

The civil government changes, however, resulted in little real local autonomy. The bill put stringent restrictions on suffrage and set property and educational qualifications for office-holding. Puerto Rico was made a part of the second judicial district of the United States with a district judge and a district attorney appointed by the President of the United States; the President was also given the authority to appoint the justices of the Puerto Rican Supreme Court. All laws passed by the

April 11, 1900, the House voted 161 to 153 to adopt in full the bill as amended by the Senate.[177]

This first skirmish in the battle over the authority of the United States to hold colonies was thus concluded by a legislative victory for the exponents of imperialism. Legislative action on Puerto Rico supported the view that Congress might exercise virtually unlimited power over the "alien" peoples of the new insular territories.[178] By avoiding the incorporation of Puerto Rico and the naturalization of its people, the legislation which emerged from Congress made possible clear-cut political and judicial tests of McKinley's expansionist policies.

III. CITIENZSHIP IN AN "UNINCORPORATED" TERRITORY: FROM THE FORAKER ACT TO THE JONES ACT (1900-1917)

The constitutional crisis precipitated by the cession of the Philippines and Puerto Rico and the congressional decision to treat both territories as colonies of the United States rather than as integral parts of the Union was resolved in the months following the enactment of the Foraker Act.[179] That landmark legislation set the stage for the presidential election of 1900; "imperialism" became the great issue of the contest between Bryan and McKinley.

Historians have doubted that "these great quadrennial convulsions can ever be a mandate on anything," [180] and it has been suggested that McKinley's impressive victory was not truly a mandate on the question that the Democratic Party platform called the "paramount" issue of the campaign.[181] Nevertheless, the fact remains that the President and the party that advocated expansion and took credit for the Foraker Act won an overwhelming victory in 1900.

House of Delegates were subject to the governor's veto; if the Puerto Rican legislature chose to override this veto, the United States Congress had an ultimate power of annulment. Thus, narrow limits were placed on the amount of self-government Puerto Rico was allowed to exercise. Foraker Act (Puerto Rico), ch. 191, 31 Stat. 77 (1900). See generally T. CLARK, supra note 70, at 6-11.

[177] 33 CONG. REC. 4071 (1900) (House vote). President McKinley signed the bill into law on April 12, 1900. See 31 Stat. 77 (1900).

[178] Congressional power to legislate for the newly acquired territories was not totally without limits however. "The guaranties of certain fundamental personal rights declared in the Constitution . . . had from the beginning full application in the Philippines and Porto Rico." Balzac v. Porto Rico, 258 U.S. 298, 312-13 (1922) (holding that the right to trial by jury was not "fundamental").

[179] Foraker Act (Puerto Rico), ch. 191, 31 Stat. 77 (1900). A civil government for the Philippines was established under the Act of July 1, 1902, ch. 1369, 32 Stat. 691 (1902).

[180] Bailey, supra note 7, at 52.

[181] NATIONAL PARTY PLATFORMS: 1840-1972, at 113 (D. Johnson & K. Porter comps. 1973).

Regardless of the "true" source of McKinley's victory the outcome of the political controversy over whether "the Constitution follows the flag" was resolved by the results of the presidential election of 1900. It was not long before the Supreme Court gave its approval to the new role of the United States as a colonial power.

A. *The Supreme Court Sanctions America's Colonial Experiment*

Judicial consideration of the constitutionality of the legislation for Puerto Rico followed shortly after the election. In the *Insular Cases, De Lima v. Bidwell,*[182] *Dooley v. United States,*[183] *Armstrong v. United States,*[184] and *Downes v. Bidwell,*[185] the Supreme Court addressed various challenges to the constitutionality of the imposition of duties on goods carried from Puerto Rico to the continental United States. These cases were argued several weeks after the presidential election and decided only two months after the second inauguration of McKinley.[186] In the view of John W. Davis the cases were "a judicial drama of truly Olympian proportions"[187] and "the most hotly contested and long continued duel in the life of the Supreme Court."[188] They reportedly stimulated stronger feelings among the justices of the Supreme Court than any case since *Scott v. Sandford* (the *Dred Scott* case).[189] In resolving these controversies the Court upheld the power of Congress to treat the islands acquired from Spain differently from the "incorporated territories." Thus, although the specific legal questions involved the imposition of customs duties, by these decisions the Supreme Court gave judicial approval to the birth of "the American Empire."[190] The Court effectively answered in the affirmative the question whether it was constitutionally permissible for the United States to possess colonies indefinitely. The decisions in the *Insular Cases,* now barely remembered by students of the Court and generations of Americans anxious to avoid the complex and somewhat unpleasant history of colonialism, prompted Finley Peter Dunne's

---

182 182 U.S. 1 (1901).

183 182 U.S. 222 (1901).

184 182 U.S. 243 (1901).

185 182 U.S. 244 (1901).

186 De Lima v. Bidwell, 182 U.S. 1 (1901), was argued on January 8-11, 1901 and decided on May 27, 1901.

187 Davis, *Edward Douglass White,* 7 A.B.A. J. 377, 378 (1921).

188 *Id.*

189 60 U.S. (19 How.) 393 (1857); Coudert, *The Evolution of the Doctrine of Territorial Incorporation,* 60 AM. L. REV. 801, 840 (1926). *See also* L. ROWE, THE UNITED STATES AND PUERTO RICO 41-42 (1904).

190 *See* Downes v. Bidwell, 182 U.S. 244, 286 (1901).

Irish-American political sage, Mr. Dooley, to expound his most famous doctrine of constitutional interpretation: "no matther whether th' constitution follows th' flag or not, the supreme coort follows th' iliction returns." [191]

In the *Insular Cases,* the Supreme Court grappled with "basic propositions of constitutional law and . . . a definition of the term 'United States' as used in the uniformity clause of the Constitution." [192] The significance of the Court's decisions for Puerto Rico was direct and lasting. The Court held that after the ratification of the Treaty of Paris and the cession of the island to the United States, Puerto Rico had ceased to be a "foreign" country within the meaning of the tariff laws.[193] Accordingly, Puerto Rico was "territory of the United States;" [194] therefore, those duties collected after the ratification of the treaty but before the enactment of the Foraker Act in 1900 were unlawfully exacted.[195] Although Puerto Rico was not a "foreign" country, neither was it a part of the United States within the terms of article I, section 8 of the Constitution,[196] which declares that "all duties, imposts, and excises shall be uniform throughout the United States." [197] It was, in the Court's view, "a territory appurtenant and belonging to the United States, but not a part of the United States within the revenue clauses of the Constitution." [198] The Foraker Act's imposition of duties upon imports from the island was therefore constitutional.

In its opinion, the Court explained that "the power to acquire territory by treaty implies, not only the power to govern such territory, but to prescribe upon what terms the United States will receive its inhabitants, and what their *status* shall be." [199] Responding to the popular notion that the Constitution followed the flag, the Court stated that this belief was due to "[t]he liberality of Congress in legislating the Constitution into all our contiguous territories [which] has undoubtedly fostered the impression that it went there by its own force." [200] The Court rejected the idea that this exten-

---

[191] F.P. Dunne, Mr. Dooley on the Choice of Law 52 (E.J. Bander ed. 1963).

[192] Coudert, *supra* note 189, at 803.

[193] De Lima v. Bidwell, 182 U.S. 1, 200 (1901).

[194] *Id.* 196.

[195] *Id.* 200; Downes v. Bidwell, 182 U.S. 244, 287 (1901).

[196] Downes v. Bidwell, 182 U.S. at 287.

[197] U.S. Const. art. I, § 8, cl. 1.

[198] Downes v. Bidwell, 182 U.S. at 287.

[199] *Id.* (emphasis supplied).

[200] *Id.* 286.

sion of the Constitution was itself constitutionally mandated, and stated that it was supported by "nothing in the Constitution itself, and little in the interpretation put upon it." [201] Finally, the Court effectively approved the retention of the newly acquired territories indefinitely. Although the opinion implied that there would be an end to colonialism at some future date, it set no limits. The essence of the philosophy of the opinion may be found in one of its final paragraphs:

> Patriotic and intelligent men may differ widely as to the desireableness of this or that acquisition, but this is solely a political question. We can only consider this aspect of the case so far as to say that no construction of the Constitution should be adopted which would prevent Congress from considering each case upon its merits, unless the language of the instrument imperatively demand[s] it. A false step at this time might be fatal to the development of what Chief Justice Marshall called the American Empire. Choice in some cases, the natural gravitation of small bodies towards large ones in others, the result of a successful war in still others, may bring about conditions which would render the annexation of distant possessions desirable. If those possessions are inhabited by alien races, differing from us in religion, customs, laws, methods of taxation and modes of thought, the administration of government and justice, according to Anglo-Saxon principles, may for a time be impossible; and the question at once arises whether large concessions ought not to be made for a time, that, ultimately, our own theories may be carried out, and the blessings of a free government under the Constitution extended to them. We decline to hold that there is anything in the Constitution to forbid such action.[202]

The significance of upholding the constitutionality of the Foraker Act was indeed great. If the Court had decided that Puerto Rico was a territory of the United States equal in status to the incorporated territories of the American West, the imposition of duties on goods carried between the island and the continental United States would have been prohibited. Although this would

---

201 *Id.*

202 *Id.* 286-87. The Court's reference to "the natural gravitation of small bodies toward larger ones" bears a striking, and probably not coincidental, resemblance to John Quincy Adams' so-called law of political gravitation; Adams had long before likened Cuba to a ripening apple destined by a kind of natural law to "gravitate only towards the North American Union." J. PRATT, A HISTORY OF UNITED STATES FOREIGN POLICY 77 (2d ed. 1965).

have deprived Puerto Rico of a source of revenue,[203] if Puerto Rico had been deemed an incorporated territory, its people arguably would have been entitled to all of the rights, privileges, and immunities guaranteed by the United States Constitution. The actual decision of the Supreme Court, however, fit much more neatly into the "large policy" of the expansionists: the power of Congress to legislate as it wished for newly acquired territories was firmly established; raw goods could be imported from Puerto Rico at lower rates of import duties than those imposed on foreign goods; and the choice of either granting Puerto Rico its independence or treating its inhabitants as equal to Americans was avoided.

In the view of the three members of the Court concurring in *Downes,* whose doctrinal approach clearly prevailed in the following years, the appropriate question was not whether Congress in legislating for the territories was subject to constitutional limitations. As Justice (later Chief Justice) White asserted, it was "self-evident" [204] that the Constitution applied to Puerto Rico; the issue was whether the specific constitutional provision relied upon was applicable.[205] Either as an incident of the right to acquire territory or the clause of article IV, section 3 of the Constitution that grants Congress the power "to dispose of and make all needful rules and regulations respecting the territory or other property of the United States," [206] the courts had long recognized a congressional "power to locally govern at discretion." [207] Because this congressional authority was founded on the Constitution, it could not properly be asserted "that the authority of Congress to govern the territories is outside of the Constitution." [208] The determination of the particular provisions of the Constitution applicable in a particular territory necessarily must be largely determined by the *status* of a territory.[209] Although certain fundamental or inherent

---

203 Funds from tariffs and duties collected on goods shipped from Puerto Rico to the United States go into the island's treasury. Jones Act, 48 U.S.C. § 734 (1976). *See* Puerto Rico v. Blumenthal, No. 75-1035 (D.C. Cir. October 7, 1978). This would not be the case if Puerto Rico were a state or incorporated territory. For the origins of this system, see notes 89-90 and 168-69 *supra* & accompanying text.

204 Downes v. Bidwell, 182 U.S. at 292 (White, J., concurring).

205 *Id.*

206 *Id.* 290.

207 *Id.*

208 *Id.*

209 *Id.* 294.

principles "which are the basis of all free government" apply to all actions of Congress in any of the territories,[210] other principles embodied in the Constitution, such as the requirement of uniformity in taxation and customs matters, would not be applicable in territories not yet incorporated into the United States.[211]

A generation later, the Supreme Court would unanimously confirm the doctrinal basis of the *Insular Cases* in *Balzac v. Porto Rico*.[212] In *Balzac,* the Court held that the constitutional status of Puerto Rico had been unaltered by the collective naturalization of its inhabitants; as a result, American citizens in Puerto Rico could not successfully assert the right to trial by jury under the sixth amendment. "It is locality that is determinative of the application of the Constitution, in such matters as judicial procedure," wrote Chief Justice Taft for a unanimous Court, "and not the status of the people who live in it." [213] Puerto Rico was not an incorporated territory, and therefore its inhabitants could claim only those constitutional rights deemed by the Court to be "fundamental." [214] United States citizenship thus would not alter the doctrine of *Downes v. Bidwell.*

The doctrine of territorial incorporation developed by the Court in the *Insular Cases* and the cases following [215] was based on precisely the same considerations that determined the nature of the 1900 legislation for Puerto Rico: an apprehension that the peoples of the new insular territories were aliens and a belief that the United States ought not to try to deal with them as though they were Americans. Like his counterparts in the executive and legislative branches of government, the principal author of the judicial doctrine of territorial incorporation, Justice White, "feared that a decision in this case in favor of the plaintiffs might be held to confer upon the citizens of the new possessions rights which could

---

210 *Id.* 291, 294.

211 [W]hilst in an international sense Porto Rico was not a foreign country, since it was subject to the sovereignty of and was owned by the United States, it was foreign to the United States in a domestic sense, because the island had not been incorporated into the United States, but was merely appurtenant thereto as a posession.

Id. 341-42.

212 258 U.S. 298 (1922).

213 *Id.* 309.

214 *Id.* 312-13.

215 Rassmussen v. United States, 197 U.S. 576 (1905) (Alaska); Dorr v. United States, 195 U.S. 138 (1904) (Philippines); Hawaii v. Mankichi, 190 U.S. 197 (1903) (Hawaii).

not be taken away from them by Congress." [216]   Moreover, there was a great concern among members of the Court, as there had been among the nation's legislators, that the decision in the Puerto Rico cases would set a precedent for the Philippines. According to Frederic R. Coudert:

> [I]n a conversation subsequent to the decision . . . [Justice White] told me of his dread lest by a ruling of the court it might have become impossible to dispose of the Philippine Islands and of his regret that one of the great parties had not adopted his doctrine of incorporation in its platform as providing the solution for the then, (as now), much mooted matter of the ultimate disposition of the Philippine Islands. It is evident that he was much preoccupied by the danger of racial and social questions of a very perplexing character and that he was quite as desirous as Mr. Justice Brown [the author of the "Opinion of the Court"] that Congress should have a very free hand in dealing with the new subject populations.[217]

The recognition by all branches of government that the people of Puerto Rico, like the Filipinos, were different from Americans, (and, therefore, that Congress ought to have a "very free hand" in developing political institutions there) was a source of considerable discomfiture to many Americans and Puerto Ricans. It was particularly distressing to those who sought to make Puerto Rico an integral part of the United States. Although the doctrine of territorial incorporation rendered colonialism constitutionally permissible, at least theoretically it left open the possibility of a change in political status. In particular, the doctrine seemed to leave open the possibility that, for one reason or another, the United States might "dispose" [218] of its insular territories. By refusing to accept the suggestion that the acquisition of new territories necessitated the immediate assimilation of alien peoples into the American system, the Court made it possible, in time, for the nation to accept the principle of self-determination free of the suggestion that statehood was the inevitable destiny of the new colonial territories.

As a result of the doctrine of territorial incorporation, the Foraker Act conferred few rights upon the people of Puerto Rico

---

216 Coudert, *supra* note 189, at 819.

217 *Id.*

218 U.S. Const. art. IV, § 3, cl. 2: "The Congress shall have the Power to *dispose* of and make all needful Rules and Regulations respecting the Territory or other Property belonging to the United States . . . ." (emphasis supplied).

"which could not be taken away from them by Congress." [219]   In the absence of a change in political status, it appeared that even American citizenship would not give Puerto Ricans any additional rights, a conclusion confirmed by the Court in *Balzac v. Porto Rico* in 1922.   There was, however, one important exception: as the Court would hold in *Balzac,* Puerto Ricans gained the right "to move into the continental United States and becoming residents of any State *there* to enjoy every right of any other citizen of the United States, civil, social and political." [220]

Following the Court's decisions in the *Insular Cases,* there were few serious doubts about the significance of American citizenship, per se, for the inhabitants of Puerto Rico.   The legislative record concerning proposals for conferring American citizenship upon the Puerto Ricans in the years after the Foraker Act and the *Insular Cases* suggests that those concerned with the subject understood that American citizenship would yield little or nothing in the way of personal rights and liberties for the inhabitants of Puerto Rico.

B. *Congressional Developments: The "Law-abiding and Industrious" People—"Two-thirds . . . White, of Spanish Origin"—of an Island "Permanently to Remain a Part of Our Territory"*

After the Supreme Court's decision in the *Insular Cases,*[221] attention began to focus on United States citizenship for Puerto Ricans not as a vehicle to secure constitutional rights for the island's people, but as a means of achieving other objectives perceived as important at the time.   American citizenship was envisioned as a way to reinforce the sense of "belonging" of a people who, unlike the Filipinos, had demonstrated no sustained resistance to American rule.   It could, and would, suggest that in the course of time and after a proper tutelage the cultural gulf between the United States and Puerto Rico might actually be narrowed or eliminated.   It could, and would, form the basis of complaints about this "second class citizenship" and of further appeals to Congress aimed at the integration of the island into the American Union.   It could, and would, constitute a formidable, if not insurmountable, obstacle to any effort, by Puerto Ricans or mainland Americans, to force the

---

[219] Coudert, *supra* note 189, at 819.   *See also* text accompanying note 139 *supra.*

[220] 258 U.S. at 308 (emphasis added).

[221] De Lima v. Bidwell, 182 U.S. 1 (1901); Dooley v. United States, 182 U.S. 222 (1901); Armstrong v. United States, 182 U.S. 243 (1901); Downes v. Bidwell, 182 U.S. 244 (1901).

United States to "dispose" of the island. All of this appears to have been perceived, at least dimly, by those who were concerned with the future of Puerto Rico, including the island's pre-eminent political leaders and, indeed, the spokesmen for its substantial, but fractious, independence movement. Interestingly enough, virtually all prominent Puerto Rican leaders whose views were recorded in the annals of Congress supported the grant of citizenship at one time or another during the period between the Foraker Act of 1900 and the Jones Act of 1917. The record suggests that congressmen interested in granting American citizenship to the Puerto Ricans could have felt that they were responding to the needs and desires of the people of Puerto Rico. There is little to indicate a purposeful design or conspiracy to impose citizenship upon a helpless or resistant people.

It is difficult, if not impossible, to ascribe to the Congress of the United States a definite viewpoint or position on a subject as complicated as that of the nation's policy toward its new colonial empire. It is possible, however, to note from the record of congressional consideration of Puerto Rican affairs in the two decades following the enactment of the Foraker Act some basic and widely-shared assumptions concerning the future development of the island and its people. Most important of all was the belief that the island was permanently to remain under the American flag.

Congressional perception of the Puerto Ricans as essentially different from the Filipinos persisted into the first two decades of the American experiment with colonialism. The race of the Puerto Ricans was the subject of some concern, especially to those members of Congress with anti-imperialist sympathies, but it was not as overtly significant a factor as in the case of the Filipinos. The apparent acceptance of colonial rule by the Puerto Ricans was also in marked contrast to the Filipino situation and undoubtedly reinforced the notion that Puerto Rico should remain permanently tied to the United States. Puerto Rican expressions of unhappiness with American colonial rule, sporadic and modest as they were, merely reinforced this notion. They generally were limited to protests concerning the limited scope of local self-government under the colonial regime—in particular, the provisions of the Foraker Act that permitted the American-appointed governor to control directly the upper house of the Puerto Rican legislature.[222] The basic

---

[222] Foraker Act (Puerto Rico) ch. 191, §§ 17, 18, 27, 31 Stat. 77 (1900). One Puerto Rican commentator notes:

[El poder legislativo de la cámara puertorriqueña] resultaba muy débil, primero por lo limitado de sus funciones en comparación con las del ejecutivo, y, en segundo lugar, porque el mismo grupo que fungía como gabinete

colonial relationship was rarely directly challenged. United States citizenship thus inevitably was considered a means of acknowledging the special place of Puerto Rico among the new colonial territories and of expressing the virtually universal expectation of a permanent relationship. And the record of Congressional inter-action with Puerto Rico's spokesmen suggests that the legislators of the new imperial state could assume that United States citizenship would be well received by the people of Puerto Rico.[223]

1. The Fifty-seventh Congress (1901-1903)

Bills granting United States citizenship to the Puerto Ricans or permitting them individually to elect citizenship were submitted to each Congress following the enactment of the Foraker Act; these proposals met with varying degrees of success. As early as the first session of Congress after passage of the Foraker Act, Delegate Flynn of Oklahoma submitted a bill "to expressly confer American citizenship upon the people of Porto Rico." [224] The Flynn bill (H.R. 15340), which would have conferred United States citizenship upon all those defined as citizens of Puerto Rico by the Foraker Act,[225] was referred to the Committee on Insular Affairs, where it died. There is no evidence regarding Delegate Flynn's purpose in introducing the bill, but it is significant that he introduced it "by request." [226] It is not known at whose request the bill was introduced, although it is possible that the request was made by Puerto Rico's first resident commissioner to the United States, Federico Degetau. In connection with H.R. 14083, the only other significant legislative proposal on Puerto Rico coming before this Congress, Commissioner Degetau made it clear that he believed the Puerto Ricans were "legally Americans." [227]

---

y jefes de Departamento intervenía mayoritariamente en la composición de la Cámara Alta. Es decir, que el ejecutivo, aparte de sus amplias atribuciones, era también la parte mas sustancial del legislativo. Por este medio se aseguraba, de un lado, una concentración de poder y al mismo tiempo que este estuviera en manos del sector extranjero.

A. SÁNCHEZ TARNIELLA NUEVO ENFOQUE SOBRE EL DESARROLLO POLÍTICO DE PUERTO RICO 98 (3d rev. ed. 1973).

223 *See* text accompanying notes 260-63, 292, 299, 300 & 398-410 *infra.* But *see* text accompanying notes 352-58 *infra.*

224 H.R. 15340, 57th Cong., 1st Sess., 35 CONG. REC. 7730 (1902) (died in committee) (text of bill on file in Library of Congress).

225 *Id.* § 1; Foraker Act (Puerto Rico), ch. 191, § 7, 31 Stat. 77 (1900).

226 H.R. 15340, *supra* note 224 (heading).

227 *Hearings on H.R. 14083 Before the House Comm. on Insular Affairs,* 57th Cong., 1st Sess. 36 (1902) [hereinafter cited as *Hearings on H.R. 14083*] (statement of Resident Comm'r Degetau).

H.R. 14083 provided for the election of a Puerto Rican "Delegate to the House of Representatives of the United States, with the right to debate, but not to vote, [and who was to be] . . . elected in lieu of the resident commissioner. . . ." [228] This delegate would enjoy "the same rights and privileges as the Delegates from the Territories of the United States." [229] Debate on the bill repeated much of the earlier congressional discussion of the Puerto Ricans and their legal status. But Representative Llewellyn Powers of Maine, who had introduced the bill, frankly admitted, in hearings before the House Committee on Insular Affairs, that he was not the author of the bill and did not know who had written it.[230] Commissioner Degetau, the only other witness to appear at the hearings on the bill, later revealed that he had drafted it.[231] In his testimony in favor of the bill, the Commissioner carefully distinguished between Puerto Rico and the Philippines. While noting "the moral influence that the passage of this bill can have on the Filipinos," [232] he observed that "Congress has the advantageous position of not being bound by it as a precedent, because of the different circumstances and conditions in which the Puerto Ricans and the Filipinos are situated toward the United States, and also by the express declarations of Congress." [233] He drew a familiar comparison: "When the generals of the American armies reached Porto Rico they found not an army that would interfere with them, but a people unanimously disposed to receive them as the heralds of institutions that had been studied and loved in Porto Rico for many years." [234]

Commissioner Degetau, along with many American legislators, evidently believed that the different response of Puerto Ricans and Filipinos to American colonial rule merited a different civil status for the inhabitants of the two territories. He noted that the Foraker Act required public officials in Puerto Rico to take an oath to support the American Constitution, whereas Filipinos were merely required to make "an oath of allegiance to the United States as a nation, exercising there military power." [235] From this fact Degetau

---

[228] H.R. Rep. No. 2158, 57th Cong., 1st Sess. 2 (1902).

[229] *Id.*

[230] *Hearings on H.R. 14083, supra* note 227, at 1 (statement of Rep. Powers).

[231] *Id.* 5 (statement of Resident Commissioner Degetau).

[232] *Id.* 4.

[233] *Id.*

[234] *Id.* (statement of Resident Commissioner Degetau).

[235] *Id.* 5.

drew the conclusion that Puerto Ricans were already virtually American citizens.

The Foraker law declared in full force and effect the orders and decrees of the military government. Moreover, the Foraker law directly provides that all officials appointed or elected under that law should take an oath to support the American Constitution. *We therefore feel that we are legally Americans,* and that as Americans we can bring to our adopted country the contribution to the common welfare that during the last century our people brought to the Spanish legislature.[236]

The bill written by Commissioner Degetau and introduced by Representative Powers was reported favorably to the House by the Committee on Insular Affairs.[237] The report echoed some of the sentiments expressed by the Commissioner and recommended the creation of the office of Delegate from Puerto Rico on grounds that later would be used to support the extension of American citizenship to the Puerto Ricans:

Porto Rico has nearly one million of inhabitants. These people are law-abiding and industrious, and in the opinion of your committee are as much entitled to have a Delegate to speak for them and represent their interests on the floor of the House of Representatives as are the less than 200,000 inhabitants of Hawaii, who now enjoy that privilege. Aside from these considerations, your committee believe that Porto Rico, because of her large business interests and important and rapidly increasing trade with the United States, and because of the admitted fact that she is permanently to remain a part of our territory, is entitled, as a matter of right, to have her representative granted the privilege of the floor of the House of Representatives where he can have suitable opportunity to voice the needs of his constituents.[238]

The House did not act on the Powers-Degetau bill, but the Commissioner's objective of obtaining direct access to the House was achieved in 1904 as a result of a change in the rules of the House

---

[236] *Id.* 4 (emphasis added). In 1903, Resident Commissioner Degetau appeared as amicus curiae before the United States Supreme Court to press the argument that Puerto Ricans were already United States citizens. *See* Gonzales v. Williams, 192 U.S. 1 (1904).

[237] H.R. REP. No. 2158, *supra* note 228, at 2.

[238] *Id.* 2.

of Representatives.[239]   Degetau's efforts in 1902, however, evoked some significant expressions of congressional perspectives on the future of Puerto Rico and its people.   These views were reflected in contemporaneous reports to the Congress by the President and the Governor of Puerto Rico.

In his first annual report to the Congress, President Theodore Roosevelt had virtually taken for granted that Puerto Rico was a permanent fixture of the American system.

> It is a pleasure to say that it is hardly more necessary to report as to Porto Rico than as to any State or Territory within our continental limits. . . .   Its people are now enjoying liberty and order under the protection of the United States, and upon this fact we congratulate them and ourselves.   Their material welfare must be as carefully and jealously considered as the welfare of any other portion of our country.[240]

The appointed governor of the island, Charles H. Allen, painted for Congress a picture of a colonial people who desired to remain permanently within the American system.   Speaking of the two political parties which had come into existence in Puerto Rico following the American occupation of the island, the Republican and Federal parties, Allen noted some significant points of similarity: "Both announce their unqualified loyalty to the United States of America; and both desire a Territorial government, in the near future, and eventually full Statehood in the American Union . . . ." [241]

In 1903, a House bill to give the resident commissioner of Puerto Rico the status of a territorial delegate was amended by the Senate on the motion of Senator Foraker.   The provisions concerning the election of a delegate were struck in favor of a section relaxing the naturalization laws "to authorize the admission to citizenship of all persons . . . [residing in Puerto Rico] who owe permanent allegiance to the United States, and who may become residents of any State or organized Territory of the United States." [242]

---

239 2 HINDS' PRECEDENTS, *supra* note 173, at § 1306.   In 1903, the House passed a bill meeting the Resident Commissioner's objectives, but the operative section was deleted from the Senate version.   H.R. 17546, 57th Cong., 2d Sess., 36 CONG. REC. 2893-94, 2987 (1903).   *See* text accompanying notes 242-44 *infra*.

240 35 CONG. REC. 86 (1901) (President's message).

241 S. Doc. No. 79, 57th Cong., 1st Sess. 45 (1901).

242 H.R. 17546, 57th Cong., 2d Sess., 36 CONG. REC. 2893 (1903).

As Senator Foraker explained, the bill would have eliminated the anomalous situation whereby Puerto Ricans, unlike aliens, were precluded from naturalization even when residing in a state or "organized Territory" of the United States, although this citizenship provision would not have affected the people of Puerto Rico generally or those individual Puerto Ricans who did not emigrate to the United States.[243]   The bill, as amended by Senator Foraker, was adopted by the Senate.[244]   Because it was passed on the final day of the session, however, there was insufficient time for the House to act on the bill.

2. The Fifty-eighth Congress (1903-1905)

The Foraker naturalization bill was presented again in the succeeding Congress [245] and was adopted by the Senate,[246] but the citizenship provision was struck by the House Committee on Insular Affairs "in view of the fact that the legal questions involved [were] about to come before the courts of the United States for authoritative decision." [247]   In the meantime, Commissioner Degetau, who now had floor privileges in the House of Representatives,[248] promptly introduced his own bill "expressly to declare the citizens of Porto Rico citizens of the United States." [249]   Although no action was taken on Commissioner Degetau's proposal, his bill effectively endorsed the various legislative efforts to obtain United States citizenship for Puerto Ricans.   These efforts were further stimulated by the position taken on the citizenship proposal by President Roosevelt in his fifth annual message to Congress on December 5, 1905: "I earnestly advocate the adoption of legislation which will explicitly confer American citizenship on all citizens of Porto Rico. There is, in my judgment, no excuse for failure to do this." [250]

---

243 Senator Foraker explained, "[The section on citizenship] simply provides that the citizens of Porto Rico may become naturalized if they wish to come here. Now they are in a worse situation than aliens, for aliens may become naturalized citizens of the United States and Porto Ricans can not." 36 CONG. REC. 2894 (1903) (remarks of Sen. Foraker).

244 *Id.* 2987 (Senate vote).

245 S. 2345, 58th Cong., 2d Sess., 38 CONG. REC. 1254 (1903).

246 *Id.*, 38 CONG. REC. at 1256 (Senate vote).

247 H.R. REP. No. 2717, 58th Cong., 2d Sess. 2 (1904).

248 *See* note 239 *supra* & accompanying text.

249 H.R. 11592, 58th Cong., 2d Sess., 38 CONG. REC. 1543 (1904).

250 40 CONG. REC. 36 (1905) (President's message).

3. The Fifty-ninth Congress (1905-1907)

Undoubtedly encouraged by President Roosevelt's support, Senator Foraker on January 4, 1906 introduced a bill "to provide that the inhabitants of Porto Rico shall be citizens of the United States." [251] The new resident commissioner from Puerto Rico, Tulio Larrínaga, followed suit on January 16, 1906. He introduced a bill that adopted in its entirety the language of Senator Foraker's citizenship bill and provided for extensive reorganization of the insular government.[252] On April 2, 1906, the chairman of the House Committee on Insular Affairs, Representative Cooper of Wisconsin, introduced a bill identical to Senator Foraker's.[253] Although none of the bills were enacted into law, hearings were held on these proposals and the Foraker and Cooper bills were favorably reported by the relevant committees of both the Senate and the House.[254] These bills set the stage for the first extended congressional discussion of American citizenship for the Puerto Ricans since the great debate on the Foraker Act in 1900.

The bill [255] sponsored by Resident Commissioner Larrínaga, who represented the dominant Union Party of Puerto Rico,[256] would have established an elective upper house for the insular legislature and provided for a variety of other reforms of the island's local government in addition to its provision extending United States citizenship to the Puerto Rican people. The bill was endorsed by the League of Municipalities of Puerto Rico, representing sixty-five of the island's sixty-six municipal governments.[257] Its

---

251 S. 2620, 59th Cong., 1st Sess., 40 CONG. REC. 682 (1906).

252 H.R. 12076, 59th Cong., 1st Sess., 40 CONG. REC. 1165 (1906) (text of bill on file in the Library of Congress).

253 The bill, as originally introduced by Representative Cooper on April 2, 1906, was indeed identical to Senator Foraker's. Subsequently, however, the text was slightly amended in committee to include mainlanders living in Puerto Rico within the definition of "the People of Porto Rico." H.R. 17661, 59th Cong., 1st Sess., 40 CONG. REC. 4627 (1906) (text of bill on file in the Library of Congress); H.R. REP. No. 4215, 59th Cong., 1st Sess. (1906).

254 S. REP. No. 2746, 59th Cong., 1st Sess. (1906); H.R. REP. No. 4215, 59th Cong., 1st Sess. (1906).

255 H.R. 12076, supra note 252.

256 The Union Party was the successor of the Federal Party. See note 241 supra & accompanying text.

257 Amendment of Porto Rican Civil Government Act, Hearings on H.R. 12076 Before the House Committee on Insular Affairs, 59th Cong., 1st Sess. 52 (1906), reprinted in COMMITTEE ON INSULAR AFFAIRS, AMENDMENT OF PORTO RICAN CIVIL GOVERNMENT ACT, COMMITTEE REPORTS, HEARINGS, AND ACTS OF CONGRESS CORRESPONDING THERETO, FIFTY-NINTH CONGRESS, 1905-1907, at 41 (1908).

spokesman, Roberto H. Todd,[258] Mayor of San Juan, was a member of the Republican Party of Puerto Rico, which favored statehood for the island. Todd offered testimony, uncontradicted by Resident Commissioner Larrínaga who accompanied him, that there were no fundamental differences between the two Puerto Rican political parties.

> The Republican Party has in its platform the aspiration that Porto Rico be ultimately admitted as a State in the Union. That is the basis of our political ambition, and no other. We do not put in anything else. The Unionists have in their platform that ambition also, as well as other ambitions. They say that as the treaty of Paris left in the hands of Congress the ultimate status of Porto Rico, they would accept anything which Congress would see fit to enact for Porto Rico. If Congress should see fit to make Porto Rico a colony, the same as the English colonies, they would accept it. If Congress saw fit to make Porto Rico a State, they would accept that also, and if Congress saw fit to make it an independent nation, they would accept that also. That is the real difference, but it is only on paper. When it comes to practice, we find that there is no difference.[259]

That there was no substantial difference at that time between the various spokesmen for Puerto Rico on such a fundamental question as citizenship was clear also from the joint resolution of the Legislature of Puerto Rico [260] that explicitly asked Congress for United States citizenship for the Puerto Ricans.[261] Additionally,

---

258 Todd is listed in some official English-language documents as *Robert* H. Todd, *see, e.g.,* J. McCLEARY, FIRST ANNUAL REGISTER OF PORTO RICO 62 (1901), but he is referred to in Spanish-language material as *Roberto* H. Todd, *see, e.g.,* A. PEDREIRA, UN HOMBRE DEL PUEBLO 137 (1937).

259 *Id.* 52.

260 At this time the House of Delegates consisted entirely of members of Commissioner Larrínaga's Union Party.

261 Joint Resolution of the Legislature of Porto Rico, *reprinted in* S. REP. No. 2746, 59th Cong., 1st Sess. 5-6 (1906). In a joint resolution of both houses, the Legislative Assembly on February 6, 1906 noted that President Roosevelt had recommended conferring American citizenship on the Puerto Ricans in his annual message to Congress and solemnly petitioned the Congress "to embody in an act the high and just recommendation made by the President in favor of granting American citizenship to the Porto Ricans." *Id.* 5. On July 10, 1906, the House of Delegates voted to send a memorial, prepared by José de Diego, to Secretary of State Elihu Root, who was then visiting San Juan. The memorial referred to the petition for United States citizenship and an elective Senate as "the supreme aspiration of all Puerto Ricans." It was to be delivered to Secretary Root by the Speaker of the House of Delegates, Rosendo Matienzo Cintrón, and a delegation which included the author of the memorial, de Diego, a Puerto Rican leader now generally identified in Puerto Rican

congressional records indicate an apparently common Puerto Rican view that United States citizenship and reform of the local government were inevitably intertwined. Mayor Todd asserted that "there is not a single Porto Rican who would not appreciate the high honor which Congress would confer upon them by . . . [extending United States citizenship]," [262] and added that "it would not take long for Congress to say that a people who could be made citizens ought to be made self-governing, because we think that one thing goes with the other." [263]

There also appears to have been no disagreement about the other factor militating in favor of extending United States citizenship to the islanders—the seemingly universal assumption, articulated by Chairman Cooper and acknowledged by Governor Beekman Winthrop, "that the United States is never going to relinquish the island." [264]

Ever anxious to distinguish between Puerto Rico and the Philippines, Senator Foraker in 1906 would explicitly state what he had merely implied during the 1900 debates on the island's first organic law—that the people of Puerto Rico had not been made citizens in 1900 solely because of the fear in Congress that it might be construed as a precedent for the treatment to be accorded to the Philippines. Foraker stated:

> It is a singular situation. We adopted section 7 of the organic act [declaring Puerto Ricans to be "citizens of Porto Rico" rather than United States citizens] because, legislating for Porto Rico before we legislated for the Philippines, we were anxious not to establish any precedent that might embarrass us in legislating for the Philippines.[265]

4. The Sixtieth Congress (1907-1909)

The citizenship proposal was revived in the following Congress by Representative Cooper, Chairman of the House Committee on

---

history texts and popular lore with leadership of the pro-independence forces within the Unionist Party. Minutes of the House of Delegates Session of July 10, 1906 (copy of typescript from archives of the Legislative Assembly of Puerto Rico in author's files). Compare his views in 1914 in text accompanying note 354 *infra.*

On de Diego as an advocate of national independence for Puerto Rico, a position seemingly at odds with his acceptance of United States citizenship for Puerto Ricans, see M. ARCE DE VÁZQUEZ, *supra* note 34, at 75-86.

[262] *Amendment of Porto Rican Civil Government Act: Hearings on H.R. 12076 Before the House Committee on Insular Affairs, supra* note 257, at 104.

[263] *Id.*

[264] *Id.* 141.

[265] *Hearings on S. 2620 Before the Senate Comm. on Pacific Islands and Porto Rico,* 59th Cong., 1st Sess. 2 (1906).

Insular Affairs, who reintroduced the bill he had sponsored during the preceding session.[266]   Three other citizenship bills were introduced during this Congress, including one by Resident Commissioner Larrínaga.[267]   In 1907 and 1908, in his annual messages to Congress, President Roosevelt reiterated his recommendation "that the rights of citizenship be conferred upon the people of Porto Rico." [268]   Although none of these proposals prospered during this Congress, Representative Cooper's bill was favorably reported by his Committee on Insular Affairs, whose members continued to view the people of Puerto Rico as "law-abiding and industrious— many of them of high intelligence and culture—and . . . entitled to be recognized as citizens of the United States." [269]   The Committee's report noted that "our people have already decided that Porto Rico is forever to remain a part of the United States," and concluded that "a people so worthy as are the inhabitants of Porto Rico, living, as they do, in territory destined forever to be under the dominion of the Government of the United States, are clearly entitled as a matter of right to be accorded the privilege and the honor of American citizenship." [270]

An expression of interest in the question of citizenship by an important American constituency found its way into the *Congressional Record* in early 1909, when Senator Du Pont of Delaware presented to the Senate a resolution, adopted at the annual meeting of the National Board of Trade, that favored United States citizenship for the Puerto Ricans because of the "earnest desire [of the people of Puerto Rico] to become more closely identified with our Government," and because "business relations between the people of the island and the people of the United States have been established upon a firm and enduring basis." [271]   The American organized labor movement soon joined the organized business community in support of the proposition that Puerto Ricans should be

---

266 H.R. 393, 60th Cong., 1st Sess., 42 CONG. REC. 19 (1907).

267 H.R. 16979, 60th Cong., 1st Sess., 42 CONG. REC. 1958 (1908). The other bills were H.R. 509, 60th Cong., 1st Sess., 42 CONG. REC. 22 (1907), introduced by Representative Douglas of Ohio; and H.R. 459, 60th Cong., 1st Sess., 42 CONG. REC. 21 (1907), introduced by Representative Hayes of California.

268 42 CONG. REC. 78 (1907) (President's message); 43 CONG. REC. 27 (1908) (President's message) (requesting "that American citizenship be conferred upon the people of Porto Rico").

269 H.R. REP. No. 1204, 60th Cong., 1st Sess. 1 (1908).

270 *Id.* 2.

271 43 CONG. REC. 2670 (1909).

American citizens,[272] and thereby reinforced the notion of the nonpartisan and noncontroversial character of the proposal.

5. The Sixty-first Congress (1909-1911)

The citizenship question came before Congress again during the first session of the Sixty-first Congress, but the two bills introduced on the subject in the House of Representatives died in committee.[273] The question of citizenship was overshadowed during this session by debate on the 1909 Olmsted amendment to the Foraker Act. This amendment provided that whenever the Puerto Rican legislature adjourned without having provided appropriations for the support of government, "an amount equal to the sums appropriated in the last appropriation bills . . . shall be deemed to be appropriated." [274]

The Olmsted amendment was passed by both houses of Congress after acrimonious debate on the government of the island; it became law on July 16, 1909.[275] The legislation was enacted in response to a governmental crisis that arose in Puerto Rico in early 1909. The island's House of Delegates (the only popularly elected chamber of Puerto Rico's legislature) [276] expressed dissatisfaction with the action of Governor Regis H. Post and the Executive Council concerning certain judicial appointments by adjourning

---

[272] The Porto Rico Free Federation of Labor, which was the insular branch of the American Federation of Labor (AFL), strongly supported American citizenship in a letter to Congress in 1909. 45 CONG. REC. 271-72 (1909). *See also* A PEOPLE WITHOUT A COUNTRY: APPEAL FOR UNITED STATES CITIZENSHIP FOR THE PEOPLE OF PORTO RICO, PUBLISHED BY THE AMERICAN FEDERATION OF LABOR, WASHINGTON, D.C., 1912, S. Doc. No. 599, 62d Cong., 2d Sess. (1912). Samuel Gompers, president of the AFL and often a spokesman in Washington for the Porto Rico Free Federation of Labor, later emphasized the support of the AFL for the citizenship provisions of the Jones Bill of 1916-1917 (H.R. 9533), although he expressed opposition to some features of the bill in a telegram to Senator Martine of New Jersey in 1917. 54 CONG. REC. 1521 (1917). For a discussion of the relationship between the Puerto Rico Free Federation of Labor and the AFL, and the support of the trade union movement for "American citizenship as a token of the permanent union of Puerto Rico and the United States and guarantee of the protection of individual rights and of the establishment of North American democratic institutions in Puerto Rico," see 1 B. PAGÁN, HISTORIA DE LOS PARTIDOS POLÍTICOS PUERTORRIQUEÑOS (1898-1956), at 175 (1972) (translation by the author).

[273] H.R. 7550, 61st Cong., 1st Sess., 44 CONG. REC. 1363 (1909) (introduced by Rep. Douglas); H.R. 96, 61st Cong., 1st Sess., 44 CONG. REC. 36 (1909) (introduced by Rep. Cooper).

[274] H.R. 9541, 61st Cong., 1st Sess., 44 CONG. REC. 1996 (1909).

[275] 44 CONG. REC. 4495 (1909). For discussion of the debate on the Olmsted bill, see text accompanying notes 280-85 *infra.*

[276] *See* note 176 *supra.*

without passing an appropriations bill for the coming year.[277]   In response to the House of Delegates' action, President Taft asked for an amendment to the Foraker Act that would enable the colonial administration in Puerto Rico to circumvent the refusal of the lower house to act on appropriations and thereby avoid similar crises in the future.[278]   The President's accusations of irresponsibility and political immaturity on the part of Puerto Rico's elected leaders—and the suggestion that too much power had been given to the Puerto Ricans "for their own good" [279]—provoked the first extended congressional debate on the island's form of government since 1900.

Proponents of the Olmsted amendment regarded the assertiveness of the House of Delegates as "[amounting] to anarchy, and . . . revolution, and nothing else"; [280] opponents of the measure noted that " '[t]he power over the purse' has been the mainstay of English liberty for a thousand years," [281] and expressed bewilderment as to "why we are called on to condemn Porto Ricans for doing the very identical thing we do ourselves in our state legislatures or Congress whenever it suits our convenience to do it." [282] Although the debate on the bill inevitably divided along traditional imperialist and anti-imperialist lines, it did not reveal any significant deviation from the basic tenets that had governed the United States' relationship with Puerto Rico since 1900: the island would permanently remain within the American system and, despite the local political dispute, the relationship was essentially trouble free. Indeed, the anti-imperialists, who might have pointed to the difficulties of colonial administration as an indication of the need to disavow colonial rule, limited their rhetoric to support of the action of the House of Delegates.   Typical of the opponents of the Olmsted amendment was Representative Borland of Missouri, who reminded the House that the Puerto Ricans had "welcomed the American arms [in 1898] and acted in cooperation with them, and . . . given

---

[277] For an account of the political crisis of 1909, see T. CLARK, *supra* note 70, at 12; 1 B. PAGÁN, *supra* note 272, at 127-43.

[278] Message from President William Howard Taft to the Congress of the United States (May 10, 1909) [hereinafter cited as Message from President Taft], *reprinted in* S. REP. No. 10, 61st Cong., 1st Sess. 1-5 (1909), *also reprinted in* H.R. REP. No. 8, 61st Cong., 1st Sess. 1-5 (1909).

[279] Message from President Taft, *supra* note 278, at 5.

[280] 44 CONG. REC. 2459 (1909) (remarks of Rep. Douglas).

[281] *Id.* 2462 (remarks of Rep. Garrett).

[282] *Id.* 2470 (remarks of Rep. Clark).

the American Government no trouble." [283]   Resident Commissioner Larrínaga, a firm opponent of the Olmsted amendment, was also at pains to underscore the good relationship that existed between Americans and Puerto Ricans. "[O]ur people take to English readily," he told the House, adding: "[F]orty years ago I was a protectionist of the American manufacturers there. I . . . built the first railroad in the island introducing American rolling stock, which cost 45 per cent higher than the European material. And I established a free school for teaching English—broken English, of course." [284]   In spite of these and other arguments against it, however, the Olmsted amendment was passed.

The question of citizenship arose only fleetingly in the course of the debate of 1909 and then only to underscore the permanent character of Puerto Rico's relationship to the United States. Thus, Representative Cooper of Wisconsin, a leading proponent of citizenship, asked whether "it is right for us permanently to retain Porto Rico because of its strategic importance and forever deny any sort of nationality to those people?" [285]

The 1909 fiscal crisis in Puerto Rico, and the ensuing congressional action to amend the Foraker Act, precipitated consideration by Congress of the state of colonial government under the island's basic law. It also effectively assured that Congress would consider more extensive legislation concerning the island's form of government, and the status of its people, shortly after enactment of the Olmsted amendment of 1909.[286]

In 1910 President Taft recommended that extensive amendments be made to the Foraker Act.[287] The President's statement prompted the introduction by Representative Olmsted of legislation designed to serve as a new fundamental law for the island.[288] Although largely concerned with the organization of the insular government, the bill adopted the recommendation of President

---

[283] *Id.* 2520 (remarks of Rep. Borland). Congressman Borland explained:

I only desire further to state that the Porto Ricans have apparently given this Government as little trouble as could be expected under any circumstances of colonial acquisition. It must be said, to the credit of Porto Rico, not only that they welcomed the advent of the Americans, but that they honestly attempted to work in harmony with the Americans.

Id.

[284] *See id.* (remarks of Resident Commissioner Larrínaga).

[285] *Id.* 2926 (remarks of Rep. Cooper).

[286] *See, e.g.,* H.R. Doc. No. 615, 61st Cong., 2d Sess. (1910) (President's message on conditions in Puerto Rico).

[287] *Id.* 1-2.

[288] H.R. 22554, 61st Cong., 2d Sess., 45 Cong. Rec. 2932 (1910) (text of bill on file in the Library of Congress).

Taft and his Secretary of War that individual Puerto Ricans be permitted to acquire citizenship voluntarily.[289]   The behavior of the House of Delegates during the fiscal crisis of 1909 apparently had a profound effect upon President Taft and the administration's allies in Congress, who now clearly believed that in Puerto Rico there was "a general and almost universal desire and demand of all classes, interests, and political parties for American citizenship for all the people of Porto Rico as a whole. . . ." [290]   Nevertheless, that idea, combined with proposals for broadening the participation of Puerto Ricans in their local government, was regarded as nothing less than "disastrous to the health and economic and political welfare of the island." [291]   Although in late December 1909 and early January 1910 the Republican and Union Parties in Puerto Rico had jointly and formally appealed to the visiting Secretary of War for "the [grant] of American citizenship to all the Porto Ricans collectively, which we consider to be an act of justice to which we deem ourselves entitled," [292] the Secretary of War preferred "to substitute for the present status an entirely new one providing for the voluntary acquirement of citizenship, with conditional suffrage rights." [293]   The purpose of the Secretary of War's proposal that an individual citizen of Puerto Rico be admitted to citizenship upon application to the courts and the taking of an oath of allegiance to the United States, combined with the additional requirement that "after a reasonable period . . . no one shall hold an elective or appointive office, or vote, who shall not be a citizen of the United States," [294] was clear enough: it would limit sharply the franchise, in a land where eighty percent of the population was illiterate and few were accustomed to judicial processes, to a relatively small number of persons.[295]

The administration's proposal for individual elective citizenship was incorporated in the bill introduced in the House on

---

289 H.R. Doc. No. 615, *supra* note 286, at 1, 4-5.

290 *Id.* 4.

291 *Id.*

292 *Id.* 3.   Similar appeals were addressed to the Secretary of War by a wide array of organizations and individuals with whom he met during his visit to the island, including island-wide and municipal officials, the Speaker of the House of Delegates, and representatives of organized labor.   The Secretary reported that "[a]ll were of the same general tenor as the one from the mayor and council of the city of Arecibo," which appealed for collective United States citizenship.   *Id.*

293 *Id.* 4-5 (remarks of Sec'y Dickinson).

294 *Id.* 5.

295 *See id.*

March 8, 1910 by Representative Olmsted [296] and was part of the bill reported favorably by his Committee on Insular Affairs one week later.[297] This bill was severely criticized by a minority of seven members of the Committee, including Resident Commissioner Larrínaga, as providing for a "scheme of government . . . even less autonomic and liberal in several of its more important features" [298] than the Foraker Act. Opposition to the bill was expressed in communications to the Congress from the House of Delegates of Puerto Rico and the leadership of both parties in Puerto Rico,[299] who nevertheless effectively expressed support for collective citizenship for Puerto Ricans. When Roberto H. Todd, Mayor of San Juan, told the Committee on Insular Affairs that "the Porto Ricans are . . . willing, in order to prove their sincerity, to accept all . . . things if they can get American citizenship," [300] not one of the Puerto Rican opponents of the bill present objected.

The report of the minority of the Committee on Insular Affairs, presented by Representative William Atkinson Jones of Virginia,[301] reminded the House of Representatives that both national political parties had promised collective citizenship to the Puerto Ricans in the 1908 general election. He noted that "aside from party pledges and other purely ethical considerations, it will impose a great hardship upon the native Porto Ricans to require them individually and separately to go through the process of naturalization." [302] In the course of the floor debate on the bill, Representative Olmsted and his Committee yielded on the question of citizenship. On June 15, 1910 the House adopted Olmsted's own amendment to provide for collective citizenship. It provided "[t]hat all citizens of Porto Rico . . . are hereby declared and shall be deemed and held to be citizens of the United States." [303] The bill, with this and other amendments, passed the House that day.[304]

---

296 H.R. 22554, *supra* note 288, at § 6.

297 H.R. REP. No. 750, 61st Cong., 2d Sess. 2-3 (1910).

298 *Id.* pt. 2, at 1.

299 *See* Letter from José de Diego, Speaker of the House of Delegates, Eduardo Giorgetti, Chairman of the Central Committee of the Union Party, and Luis Muñoz Rivera and Cayetano Coll Cuchí (the latter identified in the Congressional Record as "Cay Collcudey"), Special Commissioners to Washington from the House of Delegates. 45 CONG. REC. 7626 (1910).

300 *Id.* 8202 (remarks of Rep. Olmsted, quoting testimony of Roberto H. Todd before the House Committee on Insular Affairs).

301 H.R. REP. No. 750, *supra* note 297, pt. 2, at 1.

302 *Id.* 3.

303 45 CONG. REC. 8179, 8182 (1910).

304 *Id.* 8210 (House vote).

The Senate Committee on Pacific Islands and Porto Rico followed the lead of the House sponsors of the legislation for Puerto Rico, by initially reporting to the Senate the original Olmsted bill, including the provision for individual elective citizenship.[305] Later, after recommitment of the bill, the Committee reported the bill to the Senate, as amended on the floor of the House, to provide for collective citizenship.[306] The bill died on the floor of the Senate, following a series of procedural objections by various members and a brief substantive statement in opposition to the citizenship provision by a senator who had had much experience with colonial questions as a member of the Cabinet in the previous national administration, Senator Elihu Root of New York.[307] The effective defeat of the Olmsted bill in the Senate has been attributed to the opposition of Senator Root and to the half-hearted support given to it by the Taft administration, which was unhappy with the various House and Senate amendments broadening Puerto Rican participation in the affairs of the local government.[308] Perhaps because of his continuing displeasure with the signs of political independence shown by the elected House of Delegates, President Taft did not recommend citizenship for the Puerto Ricans in his 1909 annual message to the Congress.[309]

Thus did the first significant effort by Congress to "reform" the colonial regime in Puerto Rico come to an end.

6. The Sixty-second Congress (1911-1913)

Following the congressional elections held in 1910, in the middle of President Taft's term of office, the Senate was again organized by the Republicans. The House, however, was organized by the

---

[305] S. REP. No. 920, 61st Cong., 3d Sess. 2-3 (1910).

[306] 46 CONG. REC. 1182 (1911).

[307] *See id.* 2644-45 (remarks of Sen. Root) ("I wish now to say that I object to it . . . , [*i.e.,*] the sixth section, which confers citizenship upon the people of Porto Rico." *Id.* 2644).

[308] One writer has suggested that Root's "firm, yet quiet, opposition" was a factor in the defeat of the bill in the Senate. T. CLARK, *supra* note 70, at 21.

[309] In his annual message to Congress, President Taft stated: "The removal from politics of the judiciary by providing for the appointment of the municipal judges is excellent, and I recommend that a step further be taken by providing therein for the appointment of secretaries and marshals of these courts." 46 CONG. REC. 24 (1910) (President's message). President Taft's intention was to place the appointment power entirely out of the reach of Puerto Rican elected officials and completely in the hands of American colonial administrators. He characterized the provision in the bill for a partially elected senate—a measure that did not begin to meet the expectations of the Puerto Ricans, regardless of political party—as "of doubtful wisdom." He nonetheless described the bill as "an important measure," and recommended "its early consideration and passage." *Id.*

Democrats, and Representative Jones assumed the chairmanship of the Committee on Insular Affairs. Jones, as the ranking minority member of the Committee, had led the opposition to the restrictive provisions of the Olmsted bill of 1910, which included opposition to the provision on individual elective citizenship for the Puerto Ricans. On January 13, 1912, he introduced the first of a series of bills that envisaged collective citizenship for the Puerto Ricans.[310] One month later, Jones introduced a bill granting American citizenship to Puerto Ricans that would have permitted any person to decline American citizenship by making a declaration, under oath, of his decision to do so within six months of the effective date of the legislation before a court in his district.[311] This bill, which was reported favorably to the House of Representatives within a week of its introduction [312] and passed by the House by voice vote less than a fortnight later,[313] did not indicate whether United States citizenship would be a condition for exercising basic political rights, such as voting and holding public office. However, in another bill introduced by Jones during this Congress to reorganize the island's local government, a similar citizenship provision was included, along with a provision that after the effective date of the legislation only United States citizens would be "eligible for election or appointment to any office in Porto Rico under the Government of the United States or the Government of Porto Rico." [314] Another section would have limited the franchise after 1912 to United States citizens.[315]

Jones and his Committee were interested in providing an opportunity for dissenters in Puerto Rico to refuse United States citizenship "to avoid the possibility of its being said now, or hereafter, that American citizenship was forced upon the people of Porto Rico." [316] The intended exclusion of non-citizens of the United States from the public life of the island, however, clearly gave Puerto Ricans little real choice in the matter.

In this and other respects, the first bills introduced by Jones on the question of the citizenship of Puerto Ricans presaged the

---

310 H.R. 17836, 62d Cong., 2d Sess., 48 CONG. REC. 932 (1912).

311 H.R. 20048, 62d Cong., 2d Sess., 48 CONG. REC. 2033 (1912) (text of bill on file in the Library of Congress).

312 48 CONG. REC. 2272 (1912). See also H.R. REP. No. 341, 62d Cong., 2d Sess. (1912).

313 48 CONG. REC. 2800 (1912).

314 H.R. 24961, 62d Cong., 2d Sess. §§ 5, 33, 48 CONG. REC. 7407 (1912) (text of bill on file in the Library of Congress).

315 See id. § 34.

316 H.R. REP. No. 341, supra note 312, at 3.

legislation on the subject finally adopted in 1917. In contrast to earlier statements by proponents of citizenship on the practical effects of the naturalization of the Puerto Ricans, Jones and his Committee envisaged a political status that would accord to Puerto Ricans constitutional rights comparable to those of United States citizens residing in the Union or one of its "incorporated" territories. Thus, the Committee reported to the House that

> [t]here are many able and learned lawyers who hold that the people of Porto Rico are now citizens of the United States; that when Congress established the civil government which now exists in that island, it thereby became an [incorporated] Territory of the United States to which the Constitution of the United States is applicable as elsewhere in continental United States. But this contention, however well grounded it may be, has never received judicial or other governmental sanction either in Porto Rico or the United States, and therefore, if the people of Porto Rico are to enjoy the rights and privileges of American citizenship, it is necessary that it shall be explicitly conferred upon them by Congress.[317]

Jones and his Committee thus apparently proposed a grant of citizenship that would do substantially more than merely affirm the permanence of Puerto Rico's place under the American flag. The permanence of the association was taken for granted. Thus, the Committee could state: "It has long been a conceded fact that Porto Rico has become permanent territory of the United States."[318] The report continued:

> Its people have accepted this fact in good faith, and have never sought, nor do they desire, a separate and independent political existence. Their loyalty to the United States under all circumstances has never been questioned. What they most desire, and what they have long and earnestly endeavored to secure, is American citizenship accompanied with the right to legislate for themselves in respect to all purely local affairs. That the American people concede their right to American citizenship, and are ready and willing to accord it to them, has been frequently made abundantly manifest.[319]

---

[317] *Id.* 1.

[318] *Id.*

[319] *Id.* 1-2.

Nothing in the record suggests that Jones and his colleagues on the Committee inaccurately represented the views of the elected leadership of Puerto Rico of which they might reasonably have been aware.

In 1912, the Taft administration endorsed the Jones bill and United States citizenship for Puerto Ricans.[320] Secretary of War Henry L. Stimson, with the advice and guidance of the legal officer of his department's Bureau of Insular Affairs, Felix Frankfurter, had urged Congress to grant American citizenship to the Puerto Ricans and to disassociate citizenship from eventual statehood for the island. In his 1911 annual report to Congress, Secretary Stimson set forth the basic outlines of the proposal in words that would take on increased significance in later years:

> The demand for American citizenship on the part of Porto Ricans is genuine and well-nigh universal. It has become a deep popular sentiment, and my experience in the island convinced me that a continued refusal to grant it will gravely wound the sensibilities of this loyal people. It is a practical as well as a sentimental matter. A Porto Rican traveling abroad is literally a man without a country.
>
> I believe that the demand is just, that it is amply earned by sustained loyalty, and that it should be granted.
>
> But it is to be carefully remembered that this demand for citizenship must be, and in the minds of Porto Ricans is, entirely disassociated from any thought of statehood. It is safe to say that no substantial, approved public opinion in the United States or even in Porto Rico contemplates statehood for the island as the ultimate form of relation between us and Porto Rico. I think that the time is arriving, if it has not already arrived, when it is the part of honest and farsighted statesmanship frankly to declare our position as to the ultimate interrelation between the United States and Porto Rico so far as it is possible to do so without unduly hampering the future in wisely dealing with this problem. The connection between Porto Rico and the United States is permanent and has been from the beginning regarded as permanent. There is every reason, therefore, why the thoughts and habits of the people of both countries should as soon as possible begin to shape themselves toward the assumption of their final civil relationship.

---

[320] See 49 CONG. REC. 205, 208 (1912) (President's message).

I am of the opinion that the aim to be striven for is the fullest possible allowance of local and fiscal self-government, with American citizenship as the bond between us—in other words, a relationship analogous to the present relation between England and her over-seas self-governing territory. To my mind, this will conduce to the fullest and most self-sustaining development of Porto Rico, while at the same time it will grant to her the political and economic benefits of being under the American flag.[321]

The sentiments embodied in the report by Jones and his Committee in the House, and in the official statement by Secretary of War Stimson, were reiterated and reinforced in the favorable Senate report on the bill, issued in early 1913. In endorsing the Jones bill, the Senate Committee on Pacific Islands and Porto Rico noted that "[a]t the present time these people are in the anomalous condition of being, in their international relations, a people without a country, . . . [having] ceased to be subjects of Spain and having not become citizens of the United States." [322] Citizenship would correct this "un-American" situation [323] for a people described in the Senate report as "two-thirds . . . white, of Spanish origin" [324] and "as a whole . . . friendly to the United States and ardently desirous of the rights of citizenship." [325]

What purposes would be served by the grant of citizenship? The Senate Committee reported, somewhat ambiguously, that it would "give them certain personal legal rights and privileges both in their relations to the local government and in their status abroad; [it would] tend to increase their self-respect and to cultivate and develop a larger capacity for self-government." [326] Noting that its opponents "seem to consider that [the bill] involves the right of the inhabitants of Porto Rico to participate in the government . . . [or] that it would lead to the agitation of the question of statehood for Porto Rico," the Senate Committee specifically re-

---

[321] Annual Report to Congress by Secretary of War Henry L. Stimson, *quoted in* H.R. REP. No. 341, *supra* note 312, at 2. On Frankfurter's views in 1914, see note 33 *supra*.

[322] S. REP. No. 1300, 62d Cong., 3d Sess. 2 (1913). But of course Puerto Ricans had indeed become *subjects* or *nationals* of the United States and in that sense were not "a people without a country"; since at least 1900 they had owed allegiance to the United States and were entitled to its protection. *See* note 12 *supra*.

[323] *Id.*

[324] *Id.*

[325] *Id.*

[326] *Id.*

jected the notion that citizenship would involve "the right to participate in the government [or] affect in any particular the question of statehood." [327]

The citizenship bill was placed on the Senate calendar, where it died in early 1913.[328]   Despite the failure of the·Senate to act in the closing days of the lame duck third session of the Sixty-second Congress, it is clear that the citizenship idea, with the special gloss placed upon it by several Congresses and two successive national administrations, was now a fairly noncontroversial matter for which there was widespread, bipartisan support.

7. The Sixty-third Congress (1913-1915)

The Democratic victory in the general election of 1912 brought to power the party that in 1900 had waged a national political campaign against imperialism and thereafter had generally continued to favor liberalization of American colonial rule in the insular territories.   Nevertheless, the first Congress that met during the presidency of Woodrow Wilson devoted little attention to Puerto Rican affairs.   The only bill regarding United States citizenship for the Puerto Ricans offered during the first session of the new Congress was introduced on July 10, 1913 by Senator Poindexter of Washington.   This proposed legislation, a replica of the Jones bill of the preceding Congress, was referred to the Committee on Pacific Islands and Porto Rico chaired by Poindexter.   The bill, however, never emerged from the Committee.[329]

In his first annual message to the Congress, President Wilson held out the prospect that "[n]o doubt we shall successfully enough bind Porto Rico . . . to ourselves by ties of justice and interest and affection." [330]   Wilson envisaged "giving [the Puerto Ricans] the ample and familiar rights and privileges accorded our own citizens in our own territories"; [331] whereas for the people of the Philippines—"a more difficult and debatable matter" [332]—the United States "must hold steadily in view their ultimate independence, and we must move toward the time of that independence as steadily as the way can be cleared and the foundations thoughtfully and perma-

---

[327] Id.

[328] 49 CONG. REC. 3793 (1913).

[329] S. 2712, 63d Cong., 1st Sess., 50 CONG. REC. 2365 (1913) (text of bill on file in the Library of Congress).

[330] 51 CONG. REC. 74, 75 (1913) (President's message).

[331] Id.

[332] Id.

nently laid." [333]   The historical distinction between Puerto Rico and the Philippines was thus carried over into the Wilson administration: Puerto Rico, but not the Philippines, could and would be drawn closer to the United States; Puerto Rico, but not the Philippines, was assumed to be a permanent fixture of the American system.

In February and March of 1914, early in the second session of the Sixty-third Congress, bills were introduced in the House and in the Senate to supersede the Foraker Act with a new organic statute providing a substantially more liberal form of government for Puerto Rico.[334]   The Senate Committee on Pacific Islands and Porto Rico held hearings on the bill introduced by its new chairman, Senator Shafroth of Colorado,[335] but took no further action. In the House, the bill submitted by Representative Jones of Virginia, though favorably reported by his Committee on Insular Affairs, was not debated on the floor.[336]

The Jones bill of 1914 included the now familiar provision on collective citizenship for Puerto Ricans, with an opportunity to decline citizenship, and the additional explicit requirement that the right to vote would thereafter be limited to United States citizens.[337] Although the citizenship provision was described by the House Committee on Insular Affairs as "[p]robably the most important change made by this bill in the present law," [338] the Committee did not feel obliged to recount the now familiar reasons underlying the proposal.   It was during this period, however, that Congress for the first time was formally informed of the reservations of some Puerto Ricans concerning the proposal for collective naturalization of the islanders.

Some of those reservations were expressed, in somewhat muted terms, by Resident Commissioner Luis Muñoz Rivera.   Muñoz

---

[333] *Id.*

[334] *See* H.R. REP. No. 461, 63d Cong., 2d Sess. (1914).

[335] *Civil Government for Porto Rico: Hearings on S. 4604 Before the Senate Comm. on Pacific Islands and Porto Rico,* 63d Cong., 2d Sess. (1914) [hereinafter cited as *Hearings on S. 4604*].

[336] 51 CONG. REC. 5568 (1914).

[337] *A Civil Government for Porto Rico: Hearings on H.R. 13818 Before the House Comm. on Insular Affairs,* 63d Cong., 2d Sess. 5 (1914) [hereinafter cited as *Hearings on H.R. 13818*] (statement of Gov. Yager).   The House bill differed from the Senate version in that the latter made individual action necessary in order to *obtain* citizenship, while the former made such action necessary to *reject* citizenship. *Id.*

[338] H.R. REP. No. 461, *supra* note 334, at 2 (reference is to H.R. 14866, 63d Cong., 2d Sess. § 5, which repeats the language of H.R. 13818, 63d Cong., 2d Sess. § 5 (1914)) (text of bills on file in the Library of Congress).

Rivera had been the preeminent political figure of Puerto Rico since shortly before the American occupation of the island in 1898.[339] He had served briefly as the prime minister of the Puerto Rican government organized under the Charter of Autonomy granted by Spain in 1897 [340] and had led the dominant Union Party throughout the early American colonial period. He had served in the House of Representatives as resident commissioner—the elected representative of the people of Puerto Rico—since 1911.[341] There is no record in congressional proceedings on Puerto Rico between 1911 and 1914 that Muñoz Rivera played anything but a passive role in legislative matters. There is no evidence that he had opposed the bills offered during the Sixty-second Congress (1911-1913) that provided for citizenship for the Puerto Ricans.[342] If Muñoz Rivera's views on this subject differed from those of his two predecessors, Federico Degetau and Tulio Larrínaga, or from Representative Jones and his other colleagues on the House Committee on Insular Affairs, there is no evidence of it in congressional records prior to February 25, 1914, when he appeared before the Senate Committee on Pacific Islands and Porto Rico to urge substantially more liberal terms than those proposed by Senator Shafroth for the organization of the insular government. A provision in the Senate bill for elective citizenship, upon application by individuals, was now described by Muñoz Rivera as "liberal and generous; but there exists in Porto Rico a well-defined aspiration to the ultimate independence of the country." [343] While not identifying himself with this aspiration to ultimate independence, Muñoz Rivera for the first time raised the question whether United States citizenship might effectively foreclose that political status option:

> The majority of Porto Ricans think that conferring of American citizenship in any form whatever would interfere with the future declaration of the status of the inhabitants of the island, and I pray Congress to postpone any legislation on this point for a period of a few years so that

339 *See generally* L. Cruz Monclova, Luis Muñoz Rivera: diez años de su vida política (1959).

340 *Id.* 706.

341 47 Cong. Rec. Index, pts. 1-5, at 7 (1911).

342 *Hearings on H.R. 13818, supra* note 337, at 62.

343 *Hearings on S. 4604, supra* note 335, at 8 (statement of Resident Commissioner L. Muñoz Rivera).

we may demonstrate our capacity for self-government and Congress may fix a definite solution for the future.[344]

If Muñoz Rivera had any doubts that citizenship would preclude national independence for the island, those doubts should have vanished the day after his testimony before the Senate committee in the course of hearings on the Jones bill before the House Committee on Insular Affairs. Jones argued that if the terms of the Foraker Act were left intact, and Puerto Ricans remained "citizens of Porto Rico," there might arise some confusion about the future political status of the island: it might lead Puerto Ricans to believe "that the United States has not determined the future political status of the Porto Ricans, and they were therefore at liberty to go ahead and clamor for independence." [345] Jones asked Governor Arthur Yager:

> Do you not think that, in as much as the sentiment in the United States seems to be practically unanimous that Porto Rico is to remain permanently a part of the United States, in order to put an end to all agitation of this question there we ought to declare at once that the people of the island are citizens of the United States—that is, all who do not within a reasonable period declare that they do not wish to become such citizens? Is it not best in this way to remove this question from Porto Rican politics? [346]

As though in response to this statement by Representative Jones regarding the purpose of his bill, on the following day, February 27, 1914, Muñoz Rivera introduced a bill "to provide a civil government for Porto Rico," [347] which explicitly provided that citizens of Puerto Rico were "declared, and . . . deemed and held to be, citizens of Porto Rico and as such entitled to the protection of the United States." [348] Inasmuch as the Committee on Insular Affairs had already begun hearings on its chairman's bill on the same subject, it seems likely that Muñoz Rivera's bill was designed merely to state his position for the record.

Muñoz Rivera had another occasion to state his views on the question of citizenship when he appeared before the House Committee on Insular Affairs on March 2, 1914.

---

[344] *Id.*

[345] *Hearings on H.R. 13818, supra* note 337, at 13 (remarks of Rep. Jones).

[346] *Id.*

[347] H.R. 13979, 63d Cong., 2d Sess., 51 CONG. REC. 4065 (1914) (text of bill on file in the Library of Congress).

[348] *Id.* § 5.

The sentiments of the Porto Rican people could be con-
densed into declaring to this committee: "If you wish to
make us citizens of an inferior class, *our country not being
allowed to become a State of the Union,* or to become an
independent State, because the American citizenship
would be incompatible with any other national citizenship; *if we can not be one of your States;* if we can not constitute a country of our own, then we will have to be
perpetually a colony, a dependency of the United States.
Is that the kind of citizenship you offer us?   Then, *that
is the citizenship we refuse.*" [349]

Muñoz Rivera thus introduced the possibility of independence
for Puerto Rico—the first time that that political option appears to
have been presented to Congress by the elected representative of
the people of Puerto Rico.   But that possibility was raised only
tentatively, in the expressed desire of the dominant political force
on the island, the Union Party, to preserve independence as a possible option.   But it was an option that Muñoz Rivera himself did
not necessarily claim; rather, independence was merely an option
that Congress might, in the course of time, wish to "fix [as] a definite solution." [350]   Moreover, Muñoz Rivera was quick to indicate
that, whatever might be the views of the party he led and represented in Washington, he personally entertained no doubt that
Congress could make Puerto Ricans citizens of the United States
and nevertheless be free to grant the island its independence.

My loyalty and my party demands that I proceed in accordance with the platform of the Unionist Party, whatever may be my personal convictions in this matter . . . .

    . . . .

It seems to me that by granting to the Porto Ricans
American citizenship the Congress of the United States
will not deprive itself of the right to later grant to Porto
Rico full independence.   It seems to me that Congress of
the United States is supreme under all circumstances.
They could grant the Porto Ricans statehood or some kind
of national independence.
But a great number of my constituents do not coin-
cide with my own opinions.   I am here to represent the

---

[349] *Hearings on H.R. 13818, supra* note 337, at 54 (statement of Resident
Commissioner Luis M. Rivera [*sic*]) (emphasis added).

[350] *Hearings on S. 4604, supra* note 335, at 8 (statement of Resident Commissioner L. Muñoz Rivera).

Porto Rican people; I am not here to represent my own personal ideas.[351]

In a memorable document addressed to the President and to the Congress, Puerto Rico's House of Delegates reinforced the official position stated by Muñoz Rivera. The memorial of the House of Delegates, which was read into the *Congressional Record* by Representative McKenzie of Illinois on April 15, 1914 [352] and later also published in the record of the Senate hearings on the Shafroth bill,[353] was a notable reversal of the Puerto Rican legislature's previous statements on the subject of United States citizenship. The long and emotive statement, signed by the Speaker of the House of Delegates, José de Diego, expressed a preference for citizenship of Puerto Rico and stated, "firmly and loyally," its "opposition to being declared, in defiance of our express wish or without our express consent, citizens of any country whatsoever other than our own beloved soil." [354] It rejected the frequently stated notion that Puerto Ricans were a people without a country and that United States citizenship would afford them a more precise or clear international standing.

> We are citizens of Porto Rico and as such entitled to the protection of the United States . . . .
> American citizenship in foreign countries accords no other privilege than that of the enjoyment of the protection afforded by the Government of the United States in the extraterritoriality of consular and diplomatic law. As citizens of Porto Rico we enjoy that protection and with it the only privilege derived from American citizenship in international relationship.[355]

The memorial flatly rejected the often repeated view "that although the granting of American citizenship to Porto Ricans solves no practical problem, it yet satisfies a spiritual longing that responds to a general sentiment." [356] It noted that Congress might have mis-

---

[351] *Hearings on H.R. 13818, supra* note 337, at 56-57 (statement of Resident Commissioner Luis M. Rivera [*sic*]).

[352] 51 CONG. REC. app. 358 (1914) (remarks of Rep. McKenzie).

[353] *Hearings on S. 4604, supra* note 335, at 50-53.

[354] 51 CONG. REC. app. 358 (1914) (remarks of Rep. McKenzie). For a startlingly different view of American citizenship by the same statesman just five years earlier, see note 272 *supra*.

[355] 51 CONG. REC. app. 358 (1914) (remarks of Rep. McKenzie). *See* S. Doc. No. 599, note 272 *supra;* note 12 *supra;* note 322 *supra* & accompanying text.

[356] *Id.* 359.

interpreted "our displeasure and our protest as due to the fact that you have not granted us American citizenship." [357]   It ended with a remarkable peroration.

> And so great is our love for our own citizenship, our own fatherland, that, in conclusion, we must make use of a hyperbole to express the earnestness of our sentiment. We, like all Porto Ricans, are believers in the existence of God and of a perpetual superhuman life; but were there a citizenship of heaven with a right to eternal happiness, and it were offered us in exchange for our own, we would vacillate to accept it and should under no circumstances accept it until after death.[358]

Remarkable and nationalistic as this memorial was, it nevertheless did not appeal for independence. The failure of the document to state what its authors might want for Puerto Rico's future, combined with the ambiguities of Muñoz Rivera's testimony, could not have left Congress with a clear impression of the situation in Puerto Rico. Moreover, Muñoz Rivera's opposition to the citizenship provision of the Jones bill of 1914 was based upon the formalism of the Union Party platform, from which (to some extent) he personally disassociated himself; consequently, his opposition to the citizenship idea must be regarded as quite nominal. While noting that his constituents believed that "the granting of citizenship will interfere with their aspirations for independence," [359] he was quick to add a personal reservation and then leave the matter entirely in the hands of Jones and the Committee.

> I can not be in opposition here with the views of my people, and I leave it to the committee, which has great capacity to study it and pass upon it, and to recommend to the House of Representatives, the best thing the committee thinks ought to be done in this case.[360]

To be sure, when confronted with a request that he express a preference between statehood and national independence as the ultimate political status of the islands, Muñoz Rivera expressed a preference for independence.[361] But he then characterized inde-

---

[357] *Id.*

[358] *Id.*

[359] *Hearings on H.R. 13818, supra* note 337, at 59 (statement of Resident Commissioner Luis M. Rivera [*sic*]).

[360] *Id.*

[361] *Id.*

pendence "as a question of sentiment" [362] and declared that "[t]he people of Porto Rico would accept statehood now, although the Unionist Party . . . has eliminated the matter of statehood from its platform; yet, if you tender statehood now, I, in the name of my people, accept statehood." [363]   He acknowledged that he had once favored the Olmsted citizenship bill of several years earlier [364] and, while reiterating his opposition to the Jones proposal, made it clear that he found its provisions for collective citizenship preferable to the suggestion of the Secretary of War that citizenship be granted on an individual and elective basis with public offices and voting restricted, in time, to United States citizens. [365]

If Muñoz Rivera conveyed any message of significance to the Congress in his various public statements and actions on this subject, that message was less than clear.   Muñoz Rivera left Representative Jones, who historically had been associated with efforts to reform the colonial regime in Puerto Rico, to his own devices, and Jones could thus say, without contradiction by Puerto Rico's resident commissioner, that "this talk of independence is an idle dream on the part of the Unionist Party, and . . . it would be much better to have the matter settled now, better for the Porto Rican people themselves." [366]

Given the ambiguous nature of Muñoz Rivera's public statements and of the memorial itself, it is not surprising that Jones' citizenship provision—"framed upon the idea that Porto Rico is to remain a permanent possession of the United States . . . [and designed] to settle this question and thus remove it from Porto Rican politics" [367]—was unanimously adopted by the Committee on Insular Affairs.   Jones' proposal for collective naturalization of the Puerto Ricans survived the first Puerto Rican statements of opposition to the idea.   The legislators failed to understand the real message of the memorial—that any citizenship that did not promise eventual equality in the American Union was precisely what the members of the Puerto Rican House of Delegates did not want for their people.

---

362 *Id.* 60.

363 *Id.* 61.

364 *Id.* 62.

365 *Id.* 67. Secretary of War Garrison had explained his "third plan" before the committee on February 28, 1914. *Id.* 33-34.

366 *Id.* 59 (remarks of Rep. Jones).

367 *Id.* 58.

8. The Sixty-fourth Congress (1915-1917)

Legislation to replace the Foraker Act with a new framework for the government of Puerto Rico was considered and debated still again, and finally passed, in the Sixty-fourth Congress. A bill introduced by Representative Jones on January 20, 1916 [368] was, in its author's view, not materially different in either form or substance from the Jones bill of 1914.[369] The new Jones bill was reported without dissent to the House five days after its introduction,[370] even before the completion of hearings by the Committee on Insular Affairs. As a matter of convenience, the Committee simply adopted and reprinted its report on the 1914 Jones bill "as applicable in the main to this bill." [371] The section providing for collective citizenship for the Puerto Ricans—described in 1914, and by reference in 1916, as "[p]robably the most important change made by [the] bill" [372]—was unaltered from the 1914 bill. Surprisingly, it proved to be one of the least controversial provisions of the bill introduced by Jones in 1916. After fourteen months of deliberation on the bill by both houses of the Congress, the citizenship provision enacted in 1917 was, save for a minor technical change, identical to the original Jones proposal of 1914.[373]

By 1916, the general outline of the projected reform of the Puerto Rican government was well known. The citizenship proposal, in particular, had been pending in Congress since 1900, and there was little disposition to change the direction which Jones himself had charted for the Puerto Ricans in the preceding years. Thus, when the bill was briefly raised for the first time on the floor of the House on March 13, 1916, Representative Horace Towner of Iowa, the ranking minority member of the Committee on Insular Affairs, pressed for its early consideration on the ground that "we have had this proposition under consideration for many years . . .

---

[368] H.R. 9533, 64th Cong., 1st Sess., 53 CONG. REC. 1340 (1916).

[369] H.R. REP. No. 77, 64th Cong., 1st Sess. 1 (1916).

[370] 53 CONG. REC. 1542 (1916); H.R. REP. No. 77, *supra* note 369.

[371] H.R. REP. No. 77, *supra* note 369, at 1.

[372] H.R. REP. No. 461, 63d Cong., 2d Sess. 2 (1914); H.R. REP. No. 77, *supra* note 369, at 3.

[373] The only change in the citizenship provision adopted during the 14 months of deliberation on the bill was one that permitted Puerto Ricans one year, rather than the six months provided by the original Jones Bill, to record their preference not to become citizens of the United States. The Committee evidently believed the change too minor to merit mention. Thus, although the report detailed other changes in the text of the bill, it was silent on the one-year amendment. The Committee stated simply that the changes not discussed were deemed "of such minor importance that it is not . . . necessary to specifically call attention to them." H.R. REP. No. 77, *supra* note 369, at 2.

[and] it has been made up by the committee without any regard to partisan considerations." [374]

Discussion of the citizenship proposal during this climactic Congress followed the general lines established in earlier years. Citizenship was the inevitable byproduct of the virtually universal view that Puerto Rico, unlike the Philippines, was destined to remain permanently under the American flag. Citizenship would confirm the general policy and convictions of the key policymakers on colonial questions, including the President and his administration. It would "settle" the discussion on the island concerning the island's political status. And, presumably, it would meet the expectations of the people of Puerto Rico. Finally, Congress was ready to act on the issue.

As in the case of the 1914 Jones bill, opposition to the citizenship provision was expressed by Puerto Rico's resident commissioner, Luis Muñoz Rivera, and by leaders of the island's dominant Union Party. But the statements in opposition, as in 1914, were qualified by expressions of regret that admission to the Union as a state did not appear likely in the foreseeable future and by a clear reluctance to articulate a definite political goal for the island that would be incompatible with United States citizenship. References by Puerto Rico's representatives to the possibility of national independence were tentative and equivocal. Finally, despite the initial opposition to the citizenship provisions of the bill, the citizenship proposal was endorsed by Muñoz Rivera and by the Union Party leadership in order to obtain the benefits of a more liberal basic law for the government of Puerto Rico—a step that must have suggested to members of the Congress that the earlier opposition to citizenship was no more than a pretext designed to obtain other more important legislative objectives.

The citizenship question, when considered by Congress in 1916, was so uncontroversial that neither the Senate nor House report on the Jones bill devoted any particular attention to it. The hearings on the bill and the subsequent debates on the floor of both houses of Congress provide some evidence of congressional views on the matter and congressional perceptions of Puerto Rican opinion.

At hearings held in mid-January 1916 by the House Committee on Insular Affairs, the governor of Puerto Rico, Arthur Yager, adverted to the Philippines bill then being considered by Congress, drew the now traditional distinction between the two territories,

---

[374] 53 CONG. REC. 4021 (1916) (remarks of Rep. Towner).

and arrived at some obvious conclusions concerning the citizenship provision of the Puerto Rico bill:

> We have no preamble to this bill [as in the Philippines bill, promising their eventual independence] and do not want it, but instead of that we ask that the Porto Ricans be collectively made citizens of the United States. That takes the place of the preamble of the Philippine bill and for the reason that the Philippine Islands seem to be foreordained and elected some time for separation from the United States. Porto Rico, on the other hand, will always be a part of the United States, and the fact that we now, after these years, make them citizens of the United States simply means, to my mind, that we have determined practically that the American flag will never be lowered in Porto Rico, and it is for their good, and for ours, that the American flag remains permanently in Porto Rico. In my judgment citizenship in the country should be given because it goes with the flag.[375]

Governor Yager's sentiments expressed the almost universal conviction of members of Congress. Representative Jones, during the course of these hearings, also seized upon the difference between the Philippines and Puerto Rico and noted that "[t]he purpose of the United States seems clearly to be to retain Porto Rico permanently." [376] He added: "There is no division of sentiment in the United States, so far as I am aware, on that subject. As to whether you will have Statehood or remain a Territory is a matter that remains to be decided in the future." [377]

The reasons underlying the distinction between the Philippines and Puerto Rico were identical to those articulated in Congress during the debates on the Foraker bill of 1900: race, culture, geographic proximity, economics, and the Puerto Ricans' apparent acceptance of colonial rule. Representative Towner, who as the ranking minority member of the Committee on Insular Affairs was virtually co-manager of the Jones bill in the House, introduced the Puerto Rico bill to the House by declaring, among other things, that "[n]early three-fourths of the population are white, mostly of Spanish descent." [378] Representative Huddleston of Alabama noted

---

[375] *A Civil Government for Porto Rico: Hearings on H.R. 8501 Before the House Comm. on Insular Affairs*, 64th Cong., 1st Sess. 7 (1916) [hereinafter cited as *Hearings on H.R. 8501*] (statement of Gov. Yager).

[376] *Id.* 59 (remarks of Rep. Jones).

[377] *Id.*

[378] 53 CONG. REC. 7469 (1916) (remarks of Rep. Towner).

that "entirely different conditions obtain in Porto Rico than those which obtain in the Philippines." [379] He continued, "The people of Porto Rico are of our race, they are people who inherit an old civilization—a civilization which may be fairly compared to our own." [380] And in the Senate, Senator Shafroth of Colorado, the chairman of the Senate Committee on Pacific Islands and Porto Rico, and manager of the Jones bill in the Senate, noted that "the case of Porto Rico is entirely different from that of the Philippine Islands." [381] He gave the following reasons:

> The Porto Ricans came voluntarily under our governmental system, whereas the Philippine people did not do so; and there has been a grave question in the minds of many as to whether this Nation has a right to force a people to come under its jurisdiction and become its citizens against their will.[382]

The Puerto Ricans, as Representative Towner observed, were "a peaceable, tractable, intelligent people . . . [who since] their incorporation into our territory . . . have never given this country the least trouble, nor . . . given the governors whom we have sent to them the slightest apprehension or even embarrassment." [383]

Nothing in the hearings on the Jones bill, it would seem, had altered the traditional perception of Puerto Rico and its people. Opposition to the citizenship proposal by Puerto Rico's various spokesmen had not effectively conveyed a sense of deeply-rooted resistance to the idea of United States citizenship. The testimony of Manuel Rodríguez Serra, who appeared on behalf of the Puerto Rico Bar Association and other major civic and intellecual groups, was typical. He urged the retention of Puerto Rican citizenship "because under it we may develop, we may obtain an enlargement of our governmental powers, until the ties binding us to your Nation may, by your will, disappear, and we might become absolutely independent." [384] His deferential manner clearly suggested, however, that the independence option, such as it might be, was an option to be exercised by Congress. Indeed, when he was later explicitly asked if he desired independence, he was quick to

---

379 *Id.* 8471 (remarks of Rep. Huddleston).

380 *Id.*

381 *Id.* 12792 (remarks of Sen. Shafroth).

382 *Id.*

383 *Id.* 7469 (remarks of Rep. Towner).

384 *Hearings on H.R. 8501, supra* note 375, at 73 (statement of Mr. M. Rodríguez Serra).

reply that the Bar Association had not authorized him to make such a request.[385]   Although he was authorized by the local civic organizations he represented to plead for independence, the Bar Association, the organization most readily understood and respected by his listeners, had limited his authority.   "The bar association asked me to come here to ask only for the suppression or discontinuance of the United States District Court for Porto Rico." [386]   In response to questioning by Jones and Towner, Rodríguez Serra acknowledged that six years earlier he had favored a citizenship bill and permanent annexation to the United States because he had believed it would lead to statehood; his change of heart was the result of statements by President Taft and others that citizenship and statehood were entirely different propositions.[387]

Resident Commissioner Muñoz Rivera's testimony was no less tentative and ambiguous.   While initially claiming that the adherents of the Unionist Party—sixty-one percent of the electorate— might be regarded as favoring independence, he was forced to admit that "at the present time there are very few people asking for immediate independence.   Only the associations represented by [Mr. Rodríguez Serra] want it, and they are not very great in number." [388] It is not surprising that, after some additional moments of speculation by Muñoz Rivera, Representative Austin of Tennessee should suggest to the Committee that it "go on with [its] business" because "I think it is a waste of time to talk about this independence of Porto Rico. . . .   They are not going to have independence, but are going to stay under the flag, not only this year, but for all years to come." [389]

The statement of opposition to the citizenship provision from the representative of the Union Party of Puerto Rico, Cayetano Coll Cuchí, was no more precise or firm than those of Rodríguez Serra or Muñoz Rivera.   Coll Cuchí, who identified himself as "a firm believer in independence from all points of view and considerations," [390] suggested the importance of not precluding the possibility of independence by the collective grant of United States citizenship.   But he nevertheless found it possible to defer to the judgment of his audience even on this fundamental question.

---

385 *Id.* 82.

386 *Id.*

387 *Id.* 86-87.

388 *Id.* 84-85 (statement of Resident Commissioner Luis M. Rivera [*sic*]).

389 *Id.* 85 (statement of Rep. Austin).

390 *Id.* 95 (statement of Mr. Cuchi [*sic*]).

I can say that if the United States has decided definitely and firmly that Porto Rico is going to be a part of the American nation, the time has come to declare the Porto Ricans citizens of the United States; but if such decision has not been reached, such a declaration is absolutely premature.[391]

Coll Cuchí could not have conveyed with much force the impression that United States citizenship was incompatible with the possibility of national independence, for he explained to the House Committee on Insular Affairs that "[w]hen we say that we want an independent nation, we do not mean that we want to break away from the United States."[392] Coll Cuchí continued: "I consider that the United States is formed of a number of independent nations. I believe if we could obtain that kind of independence, within the Union, that would be the fairest and best solution of the problem, and I would be very glad and happy."[393]

Coll Cuchí's colleagues in the Union Party, who had authorized him to speak in their behalf "because of . . . [his] knowledge of the language,"[394] may have entertained strong views on the question of independence and United States citizenship, but their chosen representative informed the House Committee that he desired "an independent government, . . . *like any State of the Union*,"[395] and, when asked by Representative Miller whether he preferred "complete incorporation and statehood, or complete independence from the United States,"[396] he chose statehood, a preference he then imputed to his principals:

> MR. [COLL] CUCHÍ. I have no hesitation in answering that question. I do not dare to answer it in the name of my party, but I can answer it for myself personally. I do prefer statehood to all other kinds of government, because I think at the present time it is the highest political form of government known to the public laws of the world.
>
> MR. MILLER. What do those whom you represent think about that?
>
> MR. [COLL] CUCHÍ. I think they would approach my lines pretty nearly.

391 *Id.*
392 *Id.* 98.
393 *Id.*
394 *Id.* 100.
395 *Id.* (emphasis added).
396 *Id.* (statement of Rep. Miller).

MR. MILLER. That is not what I have been led to believe by Mr. [Muñoz] Rivera.

MR. [COLL] CUCHI. I believe he has previously so stated it. If you do not understand it that way, I think that is a misunderstanding on your part.[397]

Conclusive evidence of Muñoz Rivera's halfhearted opposition to the citizenship proposal may be found in the minutes of the House Committee on Insular Affairs. Muñoz Rivera was a member of the Committee during this period,[398] and the minutes of the Committee's sessions reveal that he was permitted to offer amendments to the bill and that he actually did offer several amendments.[399] At no time, however, did Muñoz Rivera, "for the record" or otherwise, offer an amendment to the Jones bill to strike the provisions on United States citizenship.[400]

The hearings before the Senate Committee on Pacific Islands and Porto Rico were not greatly different in tone or substance from the hearings held by the House Committee. Manuel Rodríguez Serra, once again appearing in behalf of the Puerto Rico Bar Association and leading civic and intellectual entities, opposed collective citizenship because "[we] consider that the declaration of United States citizenship means the incorporation forever of Porto Rico into the United States, and therefore the destruction of our hopes of becoming at some future day an independent nation."[401]   But

---

[397] Id. (statement of Mr. Cuchi [sic]).

[398] See J. HENRY, OFFICIAL CONGRESSIONAL DIRECTORY, 62d Cong., 1st Sess. 175, 192 (1911). Although Muñoz Rivera is not listed in the directory as a member of the Committee after January, 1913, J. BELL, OFFICIAL CONGRESSIONAL DIRECTORY, 62d Cong., 3d Sess. 175, 192 (2d ed. 1913), the minutes of the Insular Affairs Committee continue to list him as a member during the 64th Congress. See, e.g., Minutes of the House Committee on Insular Affairs, 64th Cong., 1st Sess. 3 (January 12, 1916) (minutes of meetings of the House Committee on Insular Affairs on file in the Archives of the United States) [hereinafter cited as Minutes of the House Committee on Insular Affairs (1916)].

[399] Minutes of the House Committee on Insular Affairs (1916), supra note 398, at 3.

[400] It is clear from the committee minutes that although Muñoz Rivera could not vote in committee, he was empowered to propose amendments to matters under consideration and in fact did so on several occasions. Certain of his proposals involved such technical matters as the coffee tax, id. 7 (January 14, 1916), whereas others concerned more fundamental matters, including voting rights, id. 13 (January 18, 1916), and even a proposal to reform Puerto Rico's political system along parliamentary lines, id. 7 (January 14, 1916). For examples of other motions offered by Muñoz Rivera during this period, see id. 11 (January 17, 1916). None of his proposals, however, suggested withdrawal of the Jones Act provision on citizenship. Id. passim.

[401] Government for Porto Rico: Hearings on S. 1217 Before the Senate Comm. on Pacific Islands and Porto Rico, 64th Cong., 1st Sess. 35 (1916) [hereinafter cited as Hearings on S. 1217] (statement of Mr. M. Rodríguez Serra).

he thereupon qualified his statement by arguing that "the highest aspirations of the Porto Ricans are either statehood or independence" [402] and added: "I certainly believe that statehood is the best and most honorable formula of all political regime [*sic*]. It would unquestionably be a high honor for Porto Rico to be one of the States of this Union." [403] He had concluded, however, that statehood was not possible because "[e]conomical reasons"—that he did not explain—"prevent it." [404] Similarly, a statement read in behalf of the chairman of the executive committee of the Union Party, Antonio R. Barceló, who apparently had difficulty speaking English,[405] expressed concern that United States citizenship might effectively foreclose the possibility of eventual independence for the island, but only after noting that the Union Party had altered its earlier support for citizenship in the aftermath of President Taft's assertion that the granting of citizenship did not involve a promise of statehood.[406]

Another representative of the Union Party at the Senate hearings, Cayetano Coll Cuchí, while reaffirming the Union Party position of 1916 and noting that Congress in the future might be faced "with the very serious problem of unmaking 1,500,000 citizens of the United States, which is a more serious problem than making them citizens," [407] nevertheless asserted that "[w]e do not take any *systematic* stand either against or for American citizenship." [408] Opposition to the citizenship proposal, Coll Cuchí asserted, was based upon the apprehension that it would signify "perpetual incorporation into the United States of America without hope of statehood. That is, it means Porto Rico will be a colony, a perpetual colony, and of course to that we are strongly opposed." [409] But the need to reform the colonial regime established under the Foraker Act was so important, in Coll Cuchí's view, that he favored a Jones bill that included the citizenship provision rather than no bill at all. "We have been suffering so much under our form of

---

402 *Id.*

403 *Id.*

404 *Id.*

405 Antonio R. Barceló appeared before the Committee accompanied by a Mr. González Lámas. González Lámas asked for permission to read Barceló's statement for him "in order to abbreviate and save time." *Id.* 44 (statement of Mr. Gonzales Lamas [*sic*]).

406 *Id.* 44-45.

407 *Id.* 55 (statement of Mr. Cay-Coll-Cuchi [*sic*]).

408 *Id.* (emphasis added).

409 *Id.* 74.

government that we want the bill passed with American citizenship rather than not passed at all." [410]

The Jones bill was first given extended consideration on the floor of the House of Representatives on May 5, 1916—appropriately enough, just four days after the House had adopted the Jones bill for the Philippines, the preamble of which promised the Filipinos their national independence.[411] Not surprisingly, members of the House Committee on Insular Affairs, who were familiar with testimony of Puerto Rico's leaders, could report to the House that "it can probably be said that now there is very little expectation or desire in the island for independence" [412] and that even the dominant Union Party had resolved in late 1915 to "postpone all action looking toward the independence of Porto Rico, and to devote our entire efforts toward a steady activity in favor of self-government." [413] Despite a long speech by Commissioner Muñoz Rivera in which, among other things, he opposed the collective citizenship provision of the Jones bill,[414] Representative Fess of Ohio could report to the House immediately thereafter that there was no "serious" opposition to the citizenship proposal.[415]

> There is not any serious opposition that I know of, save this one objection that has been offered, that you are trying to force citizenship upon the Porto Ricans. I am sure that is not serious when once understood. This bill does not require the Porto Rican to take an oath of allegiance to make him a citizen. . . . [I]f he frets under it and does not want to be a citizen, then it is his privelege [sic] to take the step provided in this bill, to say that he does not want to be a citizen.[416]

Muñoz Rivera's address of May 5, 1916 was unusual, if not unique, for a man who, according to a House colleague, did not often attend sessions of the House "on account of his difficulty in understanding English." [417] He expressed satisfaction with the pro-

---

410 *Id.* 75.

411 Jones Act (Philippines), ch. 416, 39 Stat. 545 (1916); 53 CONG. REC. 7210-11 (1916) (House vote).

412 53 CONG. REC. 7469 (1916) (remarks of Rep. Towner).

413 The Resolution of the Union Party of Puerto Rico from which Representative Towner quoted was adopted by more than a three-to-one margin at a convention in San Juan on October 24, 1915. *Id.*

414 *Id.* 7470-73 (remarks of Resident Commissioner Rivera [sic]).

415 *Id.* 7479 (remarks of Rep. Fess).

416 *Id.*

417 *Id.* 4022 (remarks of Rep. Borland). In the earliest (and unsuccessful) effort of the promoters of the Jones bill to obtain prompt House consideration of

vision of the Foraker Act making Puerto Ricans "citizens of Porto Rico," in noting that his (and his countrymen's) earlier enthusiasm for American citizenship had been dampened by suggestions that Puerto Rico had little or no chance of achieving statehood, regardless of citizenship. The Puerto Ricans, he said, "refuse to accept a citizenship of an inferior order, a citizenship of the second class." [418] Muñoz Rivera revealed the key to the problem when he stated:

> Give us statehood and your glorious citizenship will be welcome to us and to our children. If you deny us statehood, we decline your citizenship, frankly, proudly, as befits a people who can be deprived of their civil liberties but who, although deprived of their civil liberties, will preserve their conception of honor, which none can take from them, because they bear it in their souls, a moral heritage from their forefathers.[419]

Muñoz Rivera proposed that the question of citizenship be put to a plebiscite: "It would be strange if, having refused it so long as the majority of people asked for it, you should decide to impose it by force now that the majority of the people decline it." [420] But the evidence that a majority of the Puerto Rican people opposed citizenship was circumstantial. Because Muñoz Rivera himself admitted that no vote on the matter had been taken, he presumably imputed the views of a majority of the House of Delegates to their constituents. Moreover, there is no evidence in congressional records that he or his party ever sought the advice of the Puerto Rican electorate through local initiatives.

Muñoz Rivera's address had little impact on the House debate of this long discussed subject. What little support he stimulated for his stand against the citizenship proposal was drawn from disparate quarters of the House, but none likely to have much influence on House colleagues. From the left, he won the enthusiastic and eloquent support of Representative Meyer London of New

---

the bill, Representative Borland sought assurances from its sponsors that they had consulted with Resident Commissioner Muñoz Rivera. Borland stated that Muñoz Rivera "[n]aturally . . . is very much interested in this legislation. He told me that on account of his difficulty in understanding English he did not frequently attend the sessions of the House." *Id.* *See also* A. MORALES CARRIÓN, THE LONELINESS OF LUIS MUÑOZ RIVERA (1965) (Office of the Commonwealth of Puerto Rico, Washington, D.C., Puerto Rico Booklets Series No. 1) (copy on file at the *University of Pennsylvania Law Review*).

418 53 CONG. REC. 7472 (1916) (remarks of Resident Commissioner Rivera [*sic*]).

419 *Id.*

420 *Id.*

York, a Socialist who described the citizenship proposal as "the most absurd thing that has ever been advocated." [421] He added: "You can not compel people to love you. You can not compel people who, by their elective representatives, say that they prefer to be citizens of their own island, of their own little country, to accept your citizenship." [422] London's opposition to other aspects of the bill, especially the proposal for the disenfranchisement of illiterates, was so impassioned that it threw the House into turmoil and confusion. As the price of restoring order and avoiding a possible censure by the House, London was required to apologize to the House and to agree that some of his remarks be struck from the record because, he admitted, "[a]s they stand it would seem that I advocated or suggested that when the voters of Porto Rico were deprived of the franchise they would have a right to use violence." [423]

There was also opposition to the citizenship proposal from the other end of the political spectrum. Representative Joseph G. Cannon of Illinois, the former Speaker of the House, who believed that "[t]he people of Porto Rico have not the slightest conception of self-government," [424] opposed the citizenship idea for a variety of reasons, mostly racial. He was evidently unpersuaded by the general characterizations of the Puerto Ricans as a largely white people. Noting that he had visited Puerto Rico three times, he informed the House that "Porto Rico is populated by a mixed race. About 30 percent are pure African . . . [and fully] 75 to 80 percent of the population . . . was pure African or had an African strain in their blood." [425] He favored retention of the form of government established by the Foraker Act and interpreted Commissioner Muñoz Rivera's remarks in favor of a more liberal form of government as an appeal for eventual statehood. "God forbid," he asserted to the recorded applause of his colleagues, "that in his time or mine, there should be statehood for Porto Rico as one of the United States." [426]

House consideration of the citizenship provision of the Jones bill included little or no further floor debate, and by May 22, 1916 the House had effectively taken final action on this section of the

---

[421] *Id.* 7475 (remarks of Rep. London).

[422] *Id.*

[423] *Id.* 7477.

[424] 53 CONG. REC. app. 1036 (1916) (remarks of Rep. Cannon).

[425] *Id.* See also Representative Cannon's remarks along the same lines some weeks later, 53 CONG. REC. 8458 (1916).

[426] 53 CONG. REC. app. 1037 (1916) (remarks of Rep. Cannon).

Jones bill.[427] By that day it could be noted by one member of the House that the bill not only had the unanimous support of the Committee on Insular Affairs, but also "the support, the cordial support, of the Representative of the people of Porto Rico in this House." [428] On the following day, the House finished action on various amendments without touching the citizenship provision and passed the bill by voice vote.[429]

On May 24, 1916, the Jones bill, having passed the House, was referred to the Senate Committee on Pacific Islands and Porto Rico.[430] The Committee had already held hearings on a companion measure introduced in the Senate by Senator Shafroth. The report by Senator Shafroth's Committee, published June 30, 1916, adopted the provision on citizenship of the Jones bill in full and without comment. But the Committee eliminated a provision that would have punished any person who had declared his intention not to become a citizen of the United States by prohibiting his subsequent naturalization. This provision, in the Committee's view, "was punitive in character and failed to serve any practical purpose." [431] An effort by Senator Shafroth to have the Senate begin to consider the House bill was defeated on August 18, 1916.[432] Congress was in its customary recess from September 9 to December 3. Thus, the bill could not be brought to the floor of the Senate during the remaining months of 1916. In the meantime, on November 15, 1916, during the congressional recess, Resident Commissioner Muñoz Rivera died in Puerto Rico.[433] The island was without an official representative in Washington until well after passage of the legislation in late February 1917.[434]

President Wilson, in his annual message to Congress on December 5, 1916, asserted that favorable Senate action on "the bill amending the present organic law of Porto Rico" [435] was a matter

---

427 53 CONG. REC. 8479 (1916). For the House debate on H.R. 9533, see *id.* 1753, 4021-22, 7281-82, 7468-94, 8409-25, 8457-79; 53 CONG. REC. app. 1036-37 (1916).

428 *Id.* 8466 (remarks of Rep. Austin).

429 *Id.* 8511 (House vote).

430 *Id.* 8579.

431 S. REP. No. 579, 64th Cong., 1st Sess. 6 (1916).

432 53 CONG. REC. 12792 (1916).

433 E. MOUNTJOY, OFFICIAL CONGRESSIONAL DIRECTORY, 64th Cong., 2d Sess. 125 (1st ed. 1916). *See also* note 471 *infra.*

434 Félix Córdova Dávila, Muñoz Rivera's successor as Resident Commissioner, did not formally assume the duties of office until August 18, 1917. E. MOUNTJOY, OFFICIAL CONGRESSIONAL DIRECTORY, 65th Cong., 2d Sess. 125 (2d ed. 1918).

435 54 CONG. REC. 17 (1916) (address of President Wilson).

of "capital importance." [436]   Shortly thereafter, a bipartisan commission from Puerto Rico appeared before the Senate Committee on Pacific Islands and Porto Rico to urge the Senate to take favorable action on the pending bill.[437]   Antonio R. Barceló, who would succeed Muñoz Rivera as leader of the Union Party,[438] told Senator Shafroth that if the bill, which included the provision on United States citizenship, could be passed by the Senate before the December holiday recess "it would be the finest Christmas gift that could be made to the people of Porto Rico."[439]   The memorandum submitted to the Committee by Barceló on behalf of the "Porto Rican Commission" offered no criticism whatever of the citizenship provision, although it did contain suggestions for various technical amendments to the bill.   The memorandum also underscored the bipartisan character of the commission's membership and the unanimity with which it supported the bill.[440]   Quite clearly, as far as congressional records indicate, by December 1916 Puerto Rico's spokesmen were eager to achieve the long awaited reformation of the colonial government and no longer asserted any reservations concerning the question of United States citizenship.

The congressional recess ended on December 4, 1916.   No doubt in response to the urgings of President Wilson and the spokesmen for the various political groupings in Puerto Rico, Senator Shafroth made several efforts to raise the Puerto Rico bill for early Senate consideration.   After two unsuccessful efforts earlier in the month,[441] Shafroth was finally able to gain the floor on January 13, 1917 for the commencement of debate on the Puerto Rico legislation.   His opening statement noted that there had been some division of opinion on the island on the question of United States citizenship, but that "[t]here seems in recent years to be less opposition to citizenship on the part of the Porto Rican people, so we have provided in this bill that they shall become citizens of the United States unless they . . . file with the court a declaration that they want to remain citizens of Porto Rico." [442]

436 Id.

437 Hearings on S. 1217, supra note 401, at 127-29.

438 For a discussion of Antonio R. Barceló's accession to leadership of the Union Party after the death of Muñoz Rivera, see 1 B. PAGÁN, supra note 272, at 178, 181. See generally T. CLARK, supra note 70.

439 Hearings on S. 1217, supra note 401, at 127.

440 Id. 128-29.

441 The attempts were made on January 4, 54 CONG. REC. 828, and January 8, id. 999.

442 Id. 1325 (remarks of Sen. Shafroth).   Senator Shafroth also felt compelled to explain to the Senate that "[t]he total population of Porto Rico [was] 1,118,012. The number of whites [was] 732,555, and the number of blacks 50,245." Id.

Noting the absence of Puerto Rican representation in Congress (as a result of the death of Muñoz Rivera) and the failure to adopt the new organic law, Shafroth sought repeatedly to expedite the Senate's consideration of the bill.[443] On the citizenship provision, which evoked few questions and almost no adverse commentary, Shafroth merely reminded the Senate that "the only reason it was not done in the first instance was because of the fact that we had the Philippine proposition at the same time. They did not know exactly what they wanted to do." [444] He assured the Senate that the citizenship provision met the expectations of the Puerto Rican people and noted that "we have now in Washington representatives of the Unionist Party and representatives of the Republican Party, both satisfied with this very provision of the bill." [445] The only amendment by the Senate to the citizenship provision was a technical one: Puerto Ricans would be given one year, rather than six months, in which to decide whether to decline United States citizenship.[446] Under the terms of the bill, and indeed of all versions of the Jones citizenship bill introduced after 1912,[447] only citizens of the United States would be eligible to vote [448] or hold various offices in the government of the United States or the government in Puerto Rico.[449] Thus, the bill made any such decision to decline American citizenship an effective waiver of participation in the public life of the island.

Consideration of the bill proceeded apace in the Senate during the remainder of January 1917 and through the middle of February. References to the citizenship question or even to the question of the ultimate political fate of the island, were few and far between during these debates, consumed as they were by prolonged consideration of the technicalities of a law which would serve as the constitution of a colonial people.[450] In the course of a discussion on

---

443 *Id.* 1327, 2161 (remarks of Sen. Shafroth).

444 *Id.* 2250 (remarks of Sen. Shafroth).

445 *Id.* 2251 (remarks of Sen. Shafroth).

446 *Id.*

447 H.R. 24961, 62d Cong., 2d Sess., §§ 5, 33, 34, 48 Cong. Rec. 7407 (1912); *see* text accompanying notes 114 & 115 *supra*.

448 The Act provided "that at the first election held pursuant to this Act the qualified electors shall be those having the qualifications of voters under the present law. Thereafter voters shall be citizens of the United States." Jones Act (Puerto Rico), ch. 145, § 35, 39 Stat. 951 (1917).

449 For example, noncitizens were not "eligible to election as Resident Commissioner." Jones Act (Puerto Rico), ch. 145, § 36, 39 Stat. 951 (1917).

450 For the Senate debate on H.R. 9533 during the period January 13 through February 20, 1917, see 54 Cong. Rec. 1324-29, 2162-64, 2221-23, 2248-65, 3005-11, 3069-74, 3467-79 & 3666-67.

February 10 of requirements for the franchise, however, Shafroth did have occasion to advert to the grant of collective citizenship in familiar terms: "We have denied . . . [the Porto Rican] the right of citizenship heretofore, and he has been clamoring for it. He says, 'I have got to belong to your country, and I want to be a citizen of it.' " [451]

The Senate passed the bill on February 20, 1917.[452] Conferees were promptly appointed [453] in order to reconcile the Senate and House versions of the legislation. The conference report, involving no change in the House provision on citizenship,[454] was submitted to both houses of Congress on February 23 and 24.[455] The House approved the conference report and the final version of the bill, after a final brief debate, on February 24,[456] and the Senate followed suit two days later.[457] The act of Congress, including the citizenship provision that was virtually identical to the version proposed four years earlier by Jones, was signed by President Wilson on March 2, 1917.[458]

From June 1916 until final congressional action in February 1917, the Congress had given little or no attention to the citizenship section of the Jones bill on Puerto Rico. That matter had long since been settled and required no further commentary. But a passing reference to the citizenship provision of the bill, made in the House during the final debate on the conference report by the ranking Republican member of the Committee on Insular Affairs, Representative Towner of Iowa, summarized nearly two decades of congressional debate on citizenship for the Puerto Ricans. By granting United States citizenship to the Puerto Ricans, Towner informed the House, "[w]e are conferring on them what they ought to have had years ago and what they earnestly desire—the privilege of being American citizens and being placed under the protection of our flag." [459]

---

[451] Id. 3009-10 (remarks of Sen. Shafroth).

[452] Id. 3667 (Senate vote).

[453] Id. (Senate conferees); id. 3733 (House conferees).

[454] H.R. REP. No. 1546, 64th Cong., 2d Sess. 6 (1917) (Conference report).

[455] 54 CONG. REC. 3994 (1917) (Senate); id. 4048, 4164 (House).

[456] Id. 4164-71.

[457] Id. 4271.

[458] Id. 4810.

[459] Id. 4169 (remarks of Rep. Towner). Representative Cooper of Wisconsin remarked:

We are never to give up Porto Rico for, now that we have completed the Panama Canal, the retention of the island becomes very important to the safety of the canal, and in that way to the safety of the Nation itself. It

With the promise of independence to the Filipinos in 1916, Puerto Rico became the largest of the insular territories that were regarded as permanently under the jurisdiction of the United States. In matters of citizenship, reform of colonial administration, and representation in Congress, Puerto Rico inevitably became a model of sorts for the smaller territories of the American empire. The Virgin Islands in 1927, Guam in 1950, and the Northern Mariana Islands in 1976 successfully claimed for their people the United States citizenship extended in 1917 to the people of Puerto Rico.[460]

IV. CONCLUSION

In the Jones Act of 1917[461] the Congress of the United States liberalized the structure of colonial government in Puerto Rico and granted substantially more governmental autonomy to the island than existed under the Foraker Act of 1900.[462] Simultaneously,

helps to make the Gulf of Mexico an American lake. I again express my pleasure that this bill grants these people citizenship. *Id.* 4170 (remarks of Rep. Cooper).

460 *See* H.R. REP. No. 2093, 69th Cong., 2d Sess. 1 (1927): "The people of Puerto Rico are full citizens of the United States, and your committee sees no reason why the inhabitants of the Virgin Islands should not be placed in the same category." For the rather cursory consideration of the proposal of citizenship for the Virgin Islands on the floor of the House and the floor of the Senate, see 68 CONG. REC. 2806-07 (1927); *id.* 2779; *id.* 3979-82; *id.* 4105. The question of citizenship for the people of Guam was not seriously considered until 1937. *Citizenship for Residents of Guam, Hearings Before a Subcomm. of the Senate Comm. on Territories and Insular Affairs on S. 1450,* 75th Cong., 1st Sess. (1937). At the time, B. J. Bordallo, Chairman of the House of Council of the Guam Congress, and other proponents of the citizenship bill, repeatedly invoked the precedent of Puerto Rico and the Virgin Islands. *Id.* 6, 8 & 55. The proposal was unsuccessful but was revived and adopted in 1950. Organic Act of Guam, ch. 512, § 4, 64 Stat. 384 (1950) (current version at 8 U.S.C. § 1407 (1976)); W. Tansill, Guam and Its Administration 134 (Library of Congress, Legislative Reference Service, Public Affairs Bulletin No. 95, June 1951). Writing in 1941 of the native peoples of Guam, Laura Thompson observed that "[a]ccording to the Treaty of Paris, the political status of the Chamorros [the native people of Guam] was to be defined by the American Congress. This has never been done, however, so they rank as American nationals, not as American citizens, and they are designated as 'citizens of Guam.'" L. Thompson, Guam and Its People 56-57 (American Council, Institute of Pacific Relations, Studies of the Pacific No. 8, 1941). The status enjoyed by the Puerto Ricans from 1898 until 1917—American *nationals* rather than *citizens* —was the fate of the Guamanians for 52 years. The inhabitants of American Samoa continue to be United States *nationals.* Immigration & Nationality Act, 8 U.S.C. §§ 1101(a)(21), (22) & (29) and § 1408 (1976); *see* note 12 *supra.*

On the grant of United States citizenship to the people of the Northern Marianas, see A. LEIBOWITZ, COLONIAL EMANCIPATION IN THE PACIFIC AND THE CARIBBEAN 67-104 (1976); Cabranes, *New Colony in the Pacific,* 173 THE NEW REPUBLIC 9 (1975); *The Commonwealth of the Northern Mariana Islands: A Mass Grant of United States Citizenship,* 8 U.C.D. L. REV. 453 (1975).

461 Jones Act (Puerto Rico), ch. 145, 39 Stat. 951 (1917).

462 Foraker Act (Puerto Rico), ch. 191, 31 Stat. 77 (1900).

however, Congress reaffirmed the indefinite colonial status of the island by conferring a type of citizenship on its inhabitants that strengthened Puerto Rico's ties to the United States but gave its people few of the civil and political rights normally associated with American citizenship. From the outset, the grant of American citizenship to the people of this colony was wholly divorced from the idea of "giving . . . those people any rights that the American people do not want them to have." [463] The objective of making Puerto Ricans citizens, as Senator Foraker noted as early as 1900, was merely "to recognize that Puerto Rico belongs to the United States of America." [464] The word "citizens," he reminded his colleagues, meant nothing more than "allegiance on the one hand and protection on the other." [465] Thus, a half century after the United States proclaimed the inadmissability of the ownership of persons, it affirmed its acceptance of the contemporaneous European concept of the ownership of peoples.

As far as the proponents of United States citizenship for the Puerto Ricans were concerned, however, there was no element of compulsion in the transaction.[466] The grant of citizenship was generally believed to conform to the wishes of the people of Puerto Rico.[467] Apart from isolated and usually equivocal statements of opposition, members of Congress were aware only of widespread and sustained Puerto Rican support for the proposal.[468] The only strong statement in opposition to United States citizenship from Puerto Rico was a memorial from the House of Delegates presented to Congress in 1914, three years before the Jones Act became law.[469] Yet this memorial did not argue for independence, and its significance was undercut by the subsequent approval of the Jones Act citizenship proposal by Puerto Rican leaders. Moreover, despite an unusual and eloquent statement on the floor of the House in opposition to the citizenship proposal, Puerto Rico's resident commis-

---

[463] 33 CONG. REC. 2473 (1900) (remarks of Sen. Foraker). *See* text accompanying note 139 *supra*. *See also* text accompanying notes 216-20 *supra*. Chief Justice Taft would note that the only right that citizenship conferred upon the Puerto Ricans was the right "to move into the continental United States and becoming residents of any state there to enjoy every right of any other citizen of the United States, civil, social and political." Balzac v. Porto Rico, 258 U.S. 298, 308 (1922).

[464] 33 CONG. REC. 2473 (1900) (remarks of Sen. Foraker). *See* text accompanying notes 137-39 *supra*.

[465] *See* text accompanying note 139 *supra*.

[466] *See, e.g.,* text accompanying notes 415-16, 428, 436-40, 442 & 445 *supra*.

[467] *See, e.g.,* text accompanying notes 445, 451 & 459 *supra*.

[468] *Id.*

[469] *See* notes 352-58 *supra* & accompanying text.

sioner refrained from pursuing his opposition in committee; [470] after his death, the Jones bill, with its citizenship provision intact and supported by both of the island's major parties, was hailed as his political legacy to the Puerto Rican people.[471]   After passage of the Jones Act,[472] only 288 persons took the legal steps necessary to decline United States citizenship.[473]

In short, the United States Congress that enacted the Jones Act of 1917 cannot be said intentionally to have imposed American citizenship on the people of Puerto Rico.   Although geographic [474] and racial [475] considerations were major factors in the decision to make the Puerto Ricans American citizens, the history of support for such a measure by the island's political leaders and the lack of

---

[470] *See* text accompanying notes 398-400 *supra.*

[471] *See* text accompanying notes 436-40 *supra.*   *See also* A. MORALES CARRIÓN, *supra* note 417; 1 B. PAGÁN, *supra* note 272, at 176-82.

Puerto Rico's only English-language newspaper, in reporting the death of Muñoz Rivera, prominently noted his support for American citizenship:

> Munoz was taken ill shortly after his return from Washington at the close of Congress in September. . . . He visited many places in the island, conferring with the leaders not only of the Unionist but the Republican party and in these conferences he announced his firm conviction that Congress soon would pass a bill providing for American citizenship for Porto Ricans and extending a greater degree of self-government to the Island.
>
> His desire for American citizenship and his open advocacy of it together with his insistence that nothing be done by any of the political leaders here to hinder a closer knitting of the relations of the Island and the United States at first all but startled many of his followers who were, however, convinced of the wisdom of his course and swung in line to support him.

Porto Rico Progress, November 17, 1916, at 1, col. 1 (copy on file at the *University of Pennsylvania Law Review*).

[472] The Jones Act provided, in part, that any citizen of Puerto Rico could retain his . . . political status [*i.e.*, citizen of Puerto Rico] by making a declaration, under oath, of his decision to do so within six months of the taking effect of this Act before the district court in the district in which he resides, the declaration to be in form as follows:

> "I, _____, being duly sworn, hereby declare my intention not to become a citizen of the United States as provided in the Act of Congress conferring United States citizenship upon citizens of Porto Rico . . . ."

Jones Act (Puerto Rico), ch. 145, § 5, 39 Stat. 951 (1917).

[473] T. CLARK, *supra* note 70, at 26-27; M. MALDONADO DENIS, *supra* note 34, at 109; K. WAGENHEIM, *supra* note 5.

[474] *See, e.g.,* text accompanying note 103 *supra;* notes 117 & 118 *supra.*

[475] *See, e.g.,* text accompanying note 324 *supra.*   *Cf.* text accompanying note 378 *supra* (Representative Towner of Iowa: "nearly three-fourths of the population are white, mostly of Spanish descent") and text accompanying note 380 *supra* (Representative Huddleston of Alabama: "The people of Puerto Rico are of our race . . . ."). Representative Cannon of Illinois had an altogether different view. *See* text accompanying note 425 *supra.* *See also* Senator Shafroth's statistics on race, note 442 *supra.*

resistance to American rule were equally important factors.[476]   In granting United States citizenship to the people of Puerto Rico,

---

Whatever else it may be, Puerto Rico is not a society that is preponderantly "white" under conventional North American definitions of race. *See generally* G. LEWIS, *supra* note 5, ch. 13 (1963). The statistics on race collected by the United States Department of War and later by the United States Census Bureau, based as they were upon North American notions of race, were invariably meaningless. As a 1940 guide to the island noted, "[t]he remark has often been made that on the mainland a drop of Negro blood makes a white man a Negro; while in Puerto Rico a drop of white blood makes a Negro a white man." PUERTO RICO RECONSTRUCTION ADMINISTRATION IN COOPERATION WITH THE WRITERS' PROGRAM OF THE WORKS PROGRESS ADMINISTRATION, PUERTO RICO: A GUIDE TO THE ISLAND OF BORIQUÉN 110 (1940). *See also* G. LEWIS, *supra* note 5, at 283 ("[I]n Latin America and the Caribbean one drop of 'white' blood can launch an individual on the road to social acceptance as white."). The accelerated "amalgamative process between the races" described by Professor Lewis, G. LEWIS, *supra* note 5, at 282, and others, is effectively revealed in United States census reports between 1899 and 1950 that suggested that blacks and racially mixed persons were simply vanishing in Puerto Rico. The percentage of the Puerto Rican population reported as "white" increased with each decade of colonial rule:

1899	61.8%
1910	65.5%
1920	73.0%
1930	74.3%
1940	76.5%
1950	79.7%

See U.S. BUREAU OF CENSUS, THIRTEENTH CENSUS OF THE UNITED STATES TAKEN IN THE YEAR 1910, III POPULATION, STATISTICS FOR PORTO RICO, 1192 (1913); U.S. BUREAU OF CENSUS, FOURTEENTH CENSUS OF THE UNITED STATES (1920), III POPULATION, COMPOSITION AND CHARACTERISTICS OF THE POPULATION OF THE STATES, 1196 (1922); U.S. BUREAU OF CENSUS, FIFTEENTH CENSUS OF THE UNITED STATES: 1930, OUTLYING TERRITORIES AND POSSESSIONS, 136 (1932); U.S. BUREAU OF CENSUS, SIXTEENTH CENSUS OF THE UNITED STATES: 1940, PUERTO RICO: POPULATION, BULLETIN NO. 2, CHARACTERISTICS OF THE POPULATION 2, 8 (1943); U.S. BUREAU OF CENSUS, SEVENTEENTH CENSUS OF THE UNITED STATES (1950), II CENSUS OF POPULATION: 1950, CHARACTERISTICS OF THE POPULATION, 53-26 (1953). The absurdity of trying to classify Puerto Rico's racially mixed population in terms of North American notions of race prompted this extraordinary formulation of the "vanishing Negro" thesis in a leading American encyclopedia:

It is to be observed that while the census taken in 1887 shows a black population of 76,985, and that taken in 1897 reduces the figure to 75,824, the census of 1899 further reduces the figure to 59,390. If this decrease should continue for a number of years, the black race would eventually disappear from Porto Rico unless there is an immigration of that race from the other West Indian islands in the future. This is the only island in all the West Indies where the white population is so overwhelmingly in the majority. . . . In 1910 the colored population was 34.5 per cent of the whole; in 1920 it had declined to 27.0 per cent.

22 ENCYCLOPEDIA AMERICANA 403 (1939).

Not surprisingly, by 1960 the United States Census Bureau had given up its hopeless efforts to define Puerto Ricans by the racial categories familiar to North Americans; no statistics on race were published in the 1960 and 1970 census reports. *See* 1 U.S. BUREAU OF CENSUS, U.S. CENSUS OF POPULATION: 1960, CHARACTERISTICS OF THE POPULATION, 53-25 (1963); 1 U.S. BUREAU OF CENSUS, U.S. CENSUS OF POPULATION: 1970, CHARACTERISTICS OF THE POPULATION 53-187 (1973).

[476] *See, e.g.,* text accompanying notes 116, 118, 238, 339-42, 359-66, 382-428 *supra.*

Congress intended to distinguish between the Puerto Ricans, regarded worthy of a permanent association with the United States,[477] and the Filipinos who had vigorously and "ungratefully" resisted American rule.[478] Although in retrospect this paternalism may not reflect favorably on the members of the majority supporting the Jones Act of 1917, it demonstrates that they thought of the extension of United States citizenship as a reward to the Puerto Ricans. There is no evidence that military conscription was a purpose of the legislation.[479]

Congress did, however, impose severe restrictions on the citizenship conferred on the Puerto Rican people; in spite of the protests of some Puerto Rican leaders, for the first time in history, citizenship was granted to a people without the promise of eventual statehood [480] and without the full panoply of rights guaranteed by the United States Constitution. The Supreme Court upheld this congressional action by invoking the doctrine of territorial incorporation.[481] As a result, the year after the Filipinos were promised independence, Congress felt free to grant a limited citizenship to the Puerto Ricans and thereby indefinitely extended the island's colonial status. Ironically, neither Congress nor the Court saw anything wrong in "punishing" one people with the promise of independence and "rewarding" another with continued colonialism.

Later congresses granted a greater measure of local self-government to Puerto Rico through the Elective Governor Act of 1947 [482] and the enactment of legislation in 1950 [483] giving Puerto Rico the right to draft its own constitution. "Commonwealth" status created a third alternative acceptable at least for a time to many of Puerto

---

[477] *See, e.g.,* text accompanying note 238 *supra.*

[478] *See, e.g.,* text accompanying notes 91, 101, 113-19, 152-53 & 382-83 *supra.*

[479] *See* notes 34-36, 38-46 *supra* & accompanying text.

[480] *See, e.g.,* text accompanying notes 321, 349 & 377 *supra.*

[481] *See* text accompanying notes 182-220 *supra.*

[482] Elective Governor Act of 1947, ch. 490, 61 Stat. 770.

[483] Act of July 3, 1950, Pub. L. No. 81-600, ch. 446, 64 Stat. 319 (1950). There is much literature on Puerto Rico's "commonwealth" status and its relations with the United States after the constitution that came into force on July 25, 1952. *See, e.g.,* C. FREIDRICH, PUERTO RICO: MIDDLE ROAD TO FREEDOM (1959); G. LEWIS, *supra* note 5; American Academy of Political and Social Science, *Puerto Rico: A Study in Democratic Development,* 285 ANNALS 1 (1953); Cabranes, *The Status of Puerto Rico,* 16 INT'L & COMP. L.Q. 531 (1967); Helfeld, *The Historical Prelude to the Constitution of the Commonwealth of Puerto Rico,* 21 REV. JUR. U.P.R. 135 (1952); Helfeld, *Congressional Intent and Attitude Toward Public Law 600 and the Constitution of the Commonwealth of Puerto Rico,* 21 REV. JUR. U.P.R. 255 (1952); Magruder, *The Commonwealth Status of Puerto Rico,* 15 U. PITT. L. REV. 1 (1953); notes 19-22 *supra.*

Rico's voters. But in permitting the establishment of the Commonwealth of Puerto Rico, Congress expressly disavowed any intention to alter the island's preexisting political relationship with the United States.[484]

Prolonged association, growing economic dependence, and mass migration of Puerto Ricans to and from the continental United States made possible by United States citizenship, inevitably have had significant political consequences: fully ninety-four percent of the Puerto Rican electorate voted in 1976 for political parties devoted to maintaining, in one form or another, the "indissoluble link of the citizenship of the United States."[485] The pro-statehood

---

[484] The legislative history of the commonwealth relationship leaves no doubt that Congress did not intend to change the island's political status. *See, e.g.,* H.R. REP. No. 2275, 81st Cong., 2d Sess., *reprinted in* [1950] U.S. CODE CONG. & AD. NEWS 2681 ("It is important that the nature and general scope of S. 3336 [*A Bill to Provide for the Organization of a Constitutional Government by the People of Puerto Rico,* 81st Cong., 2d Sess. (1950)] be made absolutely clear. The bill under consideration would not change Puerto Rico's fundamental political, social and economic relationship to the United States." *Id.* at 3, U.S. CODE CONG. & AD. NEWS at 2682.). *See also* S. REP. No. 1779, 81st Cong., 2d Sess. (1950). This view was shared by the executive branch of government. *See, e.g.,* H.R. REP. No. 2275, 81st Cong., 2d Sess. 5-6, *reprinted in* [1950] U.S. CODE CONG. & AD. NEWS 2681, 2684-85 (letter of Secretary of the Interior Oscar L. Chapman to Senator Joseph C. O'Mahoney, Chairman of the Senate Committee on Interior and Insular Affairs); *id.* at 8-9, U.S. CODE CONG. & AD. NEWS at 2688-89 (letter of Assistant Secretary of State Jack K. McFall to Senator Joseph C. O'Mahoney). Senator O'Mahoney said it was "fundamental that the Constitution of the United States gives the Congress complete control and nothing in the Puerto Rican constitution could affect or amend or alter that right." *Puerto Rico Constitution: Hearings Before the Senate Comm. on Interior and Insular Affairs,* 81st Cong., 2d Sess. 40 (1952). *See generally* note 22 *supra.*

[485] *See* note 28 *supra.* Proponents of commonwealth status for Puerto Rico, including more liberal versions of that status, are no less enthusiastic in proclaiming the bond of United States citizenship than the advocates of Puerto Rico's admission to the Union as a state. References to "the indissoluble link of the citizenship of the United States" are part and parcel of formal and informal definitions of "commonwealth" status. See, for example, Law. No. 1 of the Puerto Rico Legislative Assembly (December 23, 1966), P.R. LAWS ANN. tit. 16, § 844, which defined the terms of the 1967 plebiscite on political status, *see* note 17 *supra,* and which stated that a vote in favor of "commonwealth" status would constitute "authorization to develop Commonwealth in accordance with its fundamental principles to a maximum of self-government compatible with a common defense, a common market, a common currency and *the indissoluble link of the citizenship of the United States.*" *Id.* (emphasis added). A vote in favor of "commonwealth" status was also stated to mean "[t]he inviolability of common citizenship as the primary and indispensable basis of the permanent union between Puerto Rico and the United States." *Id.* The extension of United States citizenship to the Puerto Ricans in 1917 has long been regarded by statehood advocates as a major step toward the island's admission into the Union. The current governor of Puerto Rico, Carlos Romero Barceló finds in the granting of citizenship an implicit promise of statehood. Address by Governor Romero Barceló, *supra* note 19. *See also* J. CÓRDOVA, *supra* note 33; B. CORRADA DEL RÍO, PUERTO RICO FRENTE A SU PROPIO FUTURO 12 (Pamphlet of address delivered at the Puerto Rico Bar Association, February 11, 1972) (copy in author's files). Messrs. Córdova and Corrada were each elected as pro-statehood resident commissioners in the United States House of Representatives (for

party that swept to victory in 1976 proclaims that statehood in the American Union, and "first-class" citizenship identical in all respects to that of residents of the states, is the answer to "a citizenship of an inferior order, a citizenship of the second class." [486]

Citizenship "of the second class" in a colonial setting was destined to fall into disrepute in the era of decolonization and the reassertion of claims to equality by long-oppressed racial minorities in the United States. The repudiation in the United States and elsewhere of previously accepted notions of inequality and subordination, and the apparent successes of the civil rights movement in the United States and the decolonization movements in other parts of the world, inevitably reinforced those in Puerto Rico who define the goal of statehood in terms of achieving "first class" citizenship for the island's people.[487] A Congress writing laws for a compliant colonial people in 1917 extended to the Puerto Ricans a citizenship "of the second class" perpetuating their colonial status, and a citizenship that is the root of contemporary hopes and concerns about Puerto Rico's political status. It remains for a new generation of Puerto Ricans, and another Congress, to determine when, and under what circumstances, this anomalous situation will end.

1969-1973 and 1977-1981, respectively); the former was a member of the Republican Party caucus in the House, whereas the latter is a member of the Democratic Party. *See, e.g.,* C. BROWNSON, 1971 CONGRESSIONAL STAFF DIRECTORY, 382; C. BROWNSON, 1977 OFFICIAL CONGRESSIONAL DIRECTORY, 95th Cong., 1st Sess., 195.

[486] *See* 53 CONG. REC. 7472 (1916) (remarks of Resident Commissioner Luis Muñoz Rivera, May 15, 1916).

[487] *See* J. CÓRDOVA, *supra* note 25; B. CORRADA DEL RÍO, *supra* note 485. The idea of "first-class" citizenship is the basis of the political and economic theories of the current governor of Puerto Rico, who is an advocate of statehood for Puerto Rico. *See* C. ROMERO BARCELÓ, STATEHOOD IS FOR THE POOR (1978) (published originally in Spanish as LA ESTADIDAD ES PARA LOS POBRES (1973)). *See* note 19 *supra.*

About the Author

José A. Cabranes, General Counsel of Yale University, was formerly Administrator of the Office of the Commonwealth of Puerto Rico in Washington and Special Counsel to the Governor of Puerto Rico. He is a member of the New York Bar and the District of Columbia Bar. In 1965 he received the J.D. degree from Yale Law School and in 1967 the M. Litt. (International Law) degree from the University of Cambridge.